)NCILIUM

Editorial Directors

eppe Alberigo	Bologna	Italy
am Bassett	San Francisco	U.S.A.
ory Baum O.S.A.	Toronto	Canada
z Böckle	Bonn, Röttgen	West Germany
ine van den Boogaard	Nijmegen	The Netherlands
Brand	Ankeveen	The Netherlands
e-Dominique Chenu O.P.	Paris	France
dviser)		
Congar O.P. (adviser)	Paris	France
asusai Dhavamony S.J.	Rome	Italy
dviser)		
stian Duquoc O.P.	Lyon	France
ano Floristán	Madrid	Spain
de Geffré O.P.	Paris	France
rew Greeley	Chicago	U.S.A.
bert Greinacher	Tübingen	West Germany
tavo Gutiérrez Merino	Lima	Peru
dviser)		
l Huizing S.J.	Nijmegen	The Netherlands
van Iersel S.M.M.	Nijmegen	The Netherlands
-Pierre Jossua O.P.	Paris	France
s Küng	Tübingen	West Germany
é Laurentin (adviser)	Paris	France
Maldonado	Madrid	Spain
nnes Baptist Metz	Münster	West Germany
en Moltmann	Tübingen	West Germany
s Müller	Lucerne	Switzerland
nd Murphy O. Carm.	Durham, N.C.	U.S.A.
ues-Marie Pohier O.P.	Paris	France
id Power O.M.I.	Rome	Italy
l Rahner S.J. (adviser)	Munich	West Germany
gi Sartori (adviser)	Padua	Italy
vard Schillebeeckx O.P.	Nijmegen	The Netherlands
man Schmidt S.J.	Rome	Italy
id Tracy (adviser)	Chicago	U.S.A.
on Weiler	Nijmegen	The Netherlands

Lay Specialist Advisers

Luis Aranguren	Madrid/Santa Barbara, Ca.	Spain/U.S.A.
iano Caglioti	Rome	Italy
ust Wilhelm von Eiff	Bonn	West Germany
lo Freire	Geneva	Switzerland
dré Hellegers	Washington, D.C.	U.S.A.
bara Ward Jackson	New York	U.S.A.
ald Weinrich	Köln	West Germany

CONCILI

Religion in the Se

CC

Gius
Will
Greg
Fran
Anto
Paul
Mar
  (a
Yve
Mar
  (a
Chri
Cas
Clau
And
Nor
Gus
  (a
Pete
Bas
Jean
Han
Ren
Luis
Joha
Jürg
Alo
Rola
Jaco
Dav
Kar
Lui
Edv
Her
Dav
Ant

Jos
Luc
Aug
Pac
And
Bar
Har

Co

THE POOR
AND THE CHURCH

Edited by
Norbert Greinacher and
Alois Müller

A Crossroad Book
The Seabury Press • New York

1977
The Seabury Press
815 Second Avenue
New York, N.Y. 10017

Library of Congress Catalog Card Number: 77-90099
ISBN: 0-8164-03627-1
ISBN: 0-8164-2147-1 (pbk.)
Printed in the United States of America

CONTENTS

Fernando Bastos de Avila

The Church and World Hunger

IT is hardly worth repeating that hunger is a problem on a global scale. Seen as a problem, hunger can be reduced to an academic question whose solution can be entrusted to teams of well-nourished academics.

If we are going to begin to find a solution to hunger, we have to start by seeing it not as a problem, but as a scandal. To solve a problem, imagination mobilized by reason is necessary; a scandal requires the exercise of an impassioned imagination, of shame, for its elimination.

The poor, who know hunger as a humiliating reality, not as an academic problem, feel all the hypocrisy and all the imposture implicit in the euphemisms in which we wrap their problems. The approach to hunger as problem seems characterized by a preoccupation with verbal asepsis: dense, gut terms are avoided; gentle academic euphemisms are preferred. Instead of hunger, we speak of 'malnutrition', instead of the miserable poor, the underdeveloped, we prefer to speak of the 'developing' poor, as if poverty could be the way to anything.[1]

No effective action will be taken against hunger as long as there is no general acceptance of it as scandal. That means that the first question is one of perception.

The moment when humanity first became conscious of the spectre of world hunger can be placed at the beginning of the nineteen-fifties, and the person who perhaps did more than any other to alert humanity to its tragic reality was Josue de Castro.[2] More than twenty years have gone by since then, and some measures have undoubtedly been taken. They can be put into various categories.

The first category is that of assistance, bringing immediate help in dramatic situations—something not to be underestimated, since hunger cannot wait for structural solutions. These measures, however, attenuate the effects of hunger without eliminating its causes. The best

1

example, which has become symbolic, was that of Biafra in 1975: while hundreds of thousands of people reduced to the most humiliating state of starvation were being helped by the benevolence of various countries and institutions, including the Holy See, American and Russian astronauts, two hundred miles above the scene, toasted each other in champagne; that toast had cost many millions of dollars.

The next category is that of technical resources, whether directed at multiplying the quantity available for consumption or reducing the numbers of consumers. At the same time as notable advances have been made in the techniques of productivity, soil conservation and enrichment and new forms of land-use, birth-control initiatives, campaigns and methods have also increased. We live in the era of green belts and the expansion of the International Planned Parenthood Federation. Again, without underrating the value of any of these measures, we see today that they do not attack the structural causes of the famine that grips the planet. This is shown by the third category of measures: statistical measures. Never have we been in possession of such an impressive mass of quantitative data, whether on the present-day lack of nutritive elements, which for millions means a situation of endemic hunger, or the poor prospects of emerging from this situation.[3] Faced with so much accurate data at our disposal, there can be no excuse for ignorance; we are forced to recognize the plain fact that in the last twenty years the situation has got worse, not better.

What is the reason behind society's ability to live with this intolerable burden of knowledge, when society is made up of individuals who individually would not be able to see a man go hungry without helping him? The causes of this paradox lie precisely in the question of perception. All the measures I have enumerated enable us to see hunger as a problem, not as a scandal. And hunger reduced to the status of a problem is an invitation to theorize about it, not to radical action attacking its causes and roots. Information and statistics on hunger become in a strange way an object of learned consumption: they offer material for studies and dissertations, for splashes in the world press from time to time; they are subject-matter for erudite discussion at impressive international conferences, and for sympathetic commiseration around well-laden family dining-tables.

The decisive step needed is to stop seeing hunger as a problem and to try to understand it on the basis of one's own experience.[4] The poor of the affluent societies, particularly in Europe, have a chance of reaching this sort of understanding if they recall the ignominious experience of the hunger they suffered during the War, with all the humiliating degradations that brought in its train.[5] Once one evokes this experience, which is rather pushed resolutely into the background of our consciousness as a sinister ghost, it is sufficient to recall that this is the permanent, normal situation of millions of human beings, who live obsessively besieged by hunger.

HUNGER AS A FUNCTION OF THE CONSUMER SOCIETY

I cannot claim here to be making an exhaustive examination of the complex causes of the situation we have reached today: millions starving on one hand, unequalled levels of conspicuous consumption coupled with unrivalled technological means for eliminating hunger on the other. Such an analysis offers delicious fodder for the erudite disquisitions of those whose business it is to study the 'problem of hunger'. Here I start with one fact: the impossibility of eliminating hunger within the context of a consumer society. This type of society, in the process of world-wide diffusion, in all its characteristics tends only to exacerbate the contrast inherent in the situation, which, taken to its limits, has been defined as one of 'universal apartheid'.[6]

Our technological culture has, in fact, given rise to the sort of society we now call the consumer society, which, in turn, finds itself faced with problems of such magnitude that it feels compelled to turn itself over to ever greater degrees of technocracy. The technological culture could, historically, have evolved in another direction: it could have engendered a very different alternative. In fact it has evolved into the consumer society. The technological culture is now evolving into a technocratic culture which is seeking to solve its problems, to find a way out of the *impasse* it has created for itself through the exercise of reason. But technocracy exacts a price for this, and that price is the growing alienation of the poor, who are reduced to the condition of spectators of technocratic achievement. The consumer society is becoming a spectator sport, independent of the various systems and ideologies it professes. This is the most frightening form of alienation threatening society today, the most monumental repetition of 'bread and circuses', except that now, as Jacques Attali has remarked, 'there is all the time more circus and less bread'.[7]

The dominant characteristic of the consumer society is its dynamism. Its stability depends on a constantly accelerating rhythm of consumption. It is like a bicycle: if it loses speed it loses stability; if it stops, it falls over.

At the same time, we realize the impossibility of continuing this headlong rush. Warnings on the limits of natural resources become steadily more urgent. But only serious crises, like the oil crisis, can perhaps create conditions in which humanity can rediscover lost values.

The second characteristic of the consumer society, the means by which the acceleration of consumption is assured, is the exacerbation provided by a hallucinatory publicity machine which in fact amounts to a real publicity-inspired manipulation of the poor. The monstrous costs of this publicity are largely recovered by the headlong rush to consume more.[8]

In its turn, and in order to guarantee its efficacy, this publicity machine benefits from a psychological complicity which it encourages and exacerbates to the point where it can be seen to constitute the next characteristic of this type of society: in it, a person's status is defined as a function of his level of consumption. Everyone, even those with limited purchasing power, is flattered by a constant provocation to increase and sophisticate his pattern of consumption, even if this can only be done through offering credit facilities, in order to achieve prestige, social advancement and even professional success. So, possessing more, as a means to possessing still more, relegates true human values and moral criteria for governing society to an insignificant rung of consciousness. That is a generalized and freely accepted perversion of the consumer society.

The level and volume of goods on offer in no way responds to the real needs of the poor, but to a demand distorted by propaganda, which naturally concentrates on those goods whose sale produces the highest profit margin. Basic necessities, particularly basic foodstuffs, do not excite the sensibilities of market-control mechanisms, because they are not susceptible to acquisitive instinct and cannot be translated into economic demand. The starving, the marginalized, simply do not exist for the consumer society.

Finally, despite growing ecological consciousness, in order to sustain its growth rate, the consumer society continues to despoil the natural resources of the earth and to pollute its atmosphere with its detritus. Today, however, forced to proceed with greater caution, it tries to confine the ecological damage it causes as much as possible to the defenseless peripheries of the planet.

What is most serious about the consumer society, however, is not its catastrophic world-wide dynamism, but the fact that its structures are iniquitous. What is strange and dramatic is that such an observation, shocking in its directness, is absolutely obvious to those who think from the point of view of the hungry masses of the underdeveloped world. This world no longer believes in development; the theory of development fed the illusion that the poor could be divided into developed and underdeveloped by merely quantitative distinctions that could easily be ironed out with a little good will from one to the other. The developed once had the delicacy to try to arouse our enthusiasm by calling us poor in the course of development, by referring to 'developing countries'. But today we can see the tragic outcome of this illusion: the distances that separate us have never been so great or so unbridgeable. It was in the shadow of this illusion that on the one hand, the developed nations projected themselves into a truly pre-utopian phase, whereas on the other, the underdeveloped nations, or most of them, lost any sort of economic or political viability and were reduced to the contingency of seeing themselves obliged to accept a sort of protective satellite status. Today we realize that underdevelopment is not a way to anything whatsoever, because the differences between it and development are not merely quantitative but qualitative and structural. Inequality cannot be measured in terms of *per capita* income, levels of expenditure and investment. Inequality resides in the very structure of a system which requires, as the price of the super-development of the few, the undevelopability of the great anonymous majority.

There is a particular negative proof of the thesis I am trying to put forward, that it is impossible to eliminate hunger in the context of the consumer society. This planet can only show one example of rapid, large-scale eradication of hunger, and that is the example of China, where for millions hunger has been reduced to the level of a poor but decent existence. Now the most unequivocal mark of this experience is the fact that it represents the most striking alternative to, and the most massive repudiation of, the consumer society. Under force of circumstances, the Chinese experience responded to the challenge of finding new forms of human advancement, at low ecological cost and with a low level of consumption.[9] Whether we like it or not, this is the challenge that weighs ever more heavy on the whole human race, and on technological culture itself: to reduce the aim of having more to that of being more, as *Populorum Progressio* has already suggested.[10]

THE CHALLENGE TO THE CHURCH

So we have come to one conclusion: the situation of world hunger cannot be resolved within the dynamic of the consumer society, which is in turn part of a world-wide system whose very structures are unjust.

This situation constitutes a challenge. Can the Church, as institution, simply ignore it? This is the line I should now like to follow, examining the question point by point.

1. The Church is not an international agency like the FAO, whose task is to examine the problem of hunger, to produce the respective information, and to offer technical suggestions and strategic objectives

for its solution. Nor is the Church a food warehouse nor a fund of food reserves to be doled out in urgent cases of need.

2. The difficulty in going beyond focusing on hunger as a problem in order to see it as a scandal, also affects the Church. There is a risk here that the Church can be tempted to reject the challenge of hunger by saying that it is a problem that concerns all Christians.

We know the Church is us, Christians, God's poor. We know that as Christians we have both grave responsibilities and appreciable possibilities of collaboration in the response to this challenge. But the truth is that today it is the institutional Church that is called on to respond to the challenge, that the challenge is aimed at it, and the institutional Church cannot evade the challenge. This is as true as is the fact that it uses its resources to repond to particular cases of need. In these cases, it is not content with launching a general appeal for generosity to God's poor; it takes the initiative in sending immediate help.

It is easy to recognize the fallacy by reducing the scale. If a small community, a little village, say, is attacked by famine, for whatever reason, the local Church, as an institution, feels itself directly involved, institutionally committed to the situation, and participates as an institution in efforts to eradicate the situation. It happens that today the world is the 'global village' that McLuhan called it. More than this: today we are all astronauts in 'spaceship earth', and if supplies fail, for some unforeseen reason, there is no base down there to appeal to help, because we are the earth.

3. The local churches have the grave duty, as part of their prophetic mission, of denouncing the iniquity of concentration of goods in the hands of the few, the injustice in unequal distribution of resources which the humblest have helped with their sweat and their blood to create. Closer to the different realities of each situation, the local churches are better placed to speak out more accurately and more specifically. It is not their task to propose strategic alternatives, which belong to the field of technology and are beyond their area of competence and responsibility. Nor should they allow themselves to become involved in the Manichaeism of ideological confrontation; their task is to raise their voice in the name of justice, to discern what is good so as to lend it support, and what is evil so as to condemn it. They can evidently only accomplish such a mission to the extent that, free from compromise with the political and economic powers that be, they can collaborate in freeing those whose lot they share. Only the free can set free.[11]

4. It is a fact that the situation of hunger cannot be reduced to the dimensions of national problems, or even to the dimensions of a techni-

cal problem resulting from a growing lack of resources in the face of mounting world-wide demographic pressures. Furthermore, transferring the responsibility for the hunger situation on to the demographic problem can indicate a long-term strategy, but it can also hide a deception. Hunger is with us here and now, it is a present-day problem; it is now that it is devouring its defenseless victims. The solution cannot be made to wait, and must take account of a population that will inevitably grow, despite all efforts at controlling its expansion. The fact is that we are hardly concerned with a technical or demographic problem, but with a social question, in the broad sense of the term. What is at issue is a radical choice in the face of a given system and type of society.

5. If that is the central point of the question, it is the point on which the Church's attention should be fixed. On this point, the Church is in a privileged position to make an effective contribution. It is in fact present on both sides of the trench, in both camps of the conflict. It is with those who go without, the starving, the oppressed, whose needs and demands it can make explicit. It can be, and has been, the voice of those who have no voice of their own. But it is also with the affluent and the oppressors, whose consciences it can trouble with the voice of the oppressed. And it cannot abdicate from this mission without abdicating from its prophetic mission.

6. The situation of hunger has an ethical dimension, and this dimension must be of direct concern to the Church. Such a situation is not decided by lower limits, or by material and technological limitations. It is also decided by upper limits, ethical in nature, formed by the low ceiling of anti-values limiting the possibilities of choice. Adherence to patterns of high consumption, national susceptibilities, the immense investment in death represented by the arms race, the cost of maintaining organs of repression—these are some, but by no means all, of the anti-values that press heavily on humanity and limit its choices of action for solving the scandal of hunger. The institutional Church has the prophetic duty of raising its voice against all these, whereas the individual Christian is virtually powerless.

7. There is a growing dissatisfaction with grandiose official pronouncements. These are often drawn up with such a finely-balanced set of alternative recommendations that, in their anxiety not to offend any important faction, they cancel each other out and in the end amount to nothing. That is what leads me to think that, faced as it now is with the gravity of the scandal of hunger, the Church today is being challenged to advance beyond the realm of pronouncements into that of prophetic action. The prophetic act is one that places the Church at the point of no return and gives it no chance of retracting. Such an act would be one

of voluntary shedding of worldly goods, which would also have a symbolic value and place the Church firmly in a position of commitment to those who suffer injustice.

8. This should be a radical shedding, which would have to undo the preconceptions and *partis pris* preventing us from opening our minds to solutions tenaciously excluded from the horizons of the Church's thinking by a long tradition. An example of this set thinking is provided by the difficulty the Church finds in exorcising the term 'socialism', despite the profound social and semantic changes it has undergone since the first anathemas were pronounced against it. If it is impossible to eliminate hunger within the structures and dynamic of an unjust and predatory social system, then it is an ethical imperative for our age to look for, and find, an alternative system.

Such an alternative can only be defined in terms of a model whose characteristics are radically different from those of the system in force. A model free from the quantitative obsession with indefinite increase in measurable values: endless increase in *per capita* income, GNP, indices of public investment and expenditure, of industrial growth, of the number of cars on the roads, of television sets and freezers per head of population. A model dedicated to the primacy of the permanent values of 'being more', of justice, friendship and love, of truth, loyalty and beauty; a model devoted to finding new forms of human advancement and community, at a low ecological cost. 'Societies will cease their hope of indefinitely renewed progress . . . There is already a doubt creeping in about both its value and its possibility of success. What does it really mean, this endless quest for a progress that always still eludes us when we seem to have reached it? Unachieved, progress leaves us with a feeling of dissatisfaction. We are right, without a doubt, to denounce now both the limitations and the pernicious effects of purely quantitative economic growth and to be suspicious of reaching the qualitative objectives as well. The quality and truth of human relationships, the degree of responsibility and participation they offer are no less significant or important for the future of society than the quantity and variety of goods produced and consumed. Going beyond the temptation to measure everything in terms of efficiency and exchange values, and to see all relationships as ones of power and self-interest, man today wants, increasingly, to substitute these quantitative criteria by intensity of communication, diffusion of knowledge and culture, mutual service and good fellowship in order to carry out a common task together'.[12]

The model is one that will prepare the way for increasing socialization; a model in fact that is more and more insistently being called socialism with freedom. It is easy to see that the term 'socialism' is used here with a deep shift of meaning. It is not a question of socialism as an alternative political system, one more régime to take over and be ousted from power, but of socialism as a cultural alternative, with no necessary attachment to remote philosophical or doctrinal origins. John XXIII once alerted us to the opportunity for such an opening, transcending the ephemeral pettiness of doctrinaire squabbling: "It is as well not to identify false philosophical notions on the origin or end of the universe, on nature and man, with historical movements whose end is economic, social, cultural or political, even though such movements have their origins in these philosophical ideas and continue to draw inspiration from them. Doctrine, once formulated, remains what it is, but a movement, involved as it is in historical situations in a continual process of becoming, cannot help but be influenced by these, and is therefore susceptible to profound changes. Besides, who can deny that these movements, to the extent that they are guided by right reason, can contain positive elements worthy of approval?".[13]

The institutional Church cannot exempt itself from this ethical imperative of our time, and cannot fail to use the whole weight of its moral authority to encourage its sons and daughters to engage themselves in the response to this challenge. It would be disastrous if adherence to verbal stereotypes kept it aloof from this new and deep cultural transformation which with it, without it or against it, is preparing the only alternative capable of delivering mankind from the scandal of hunger.

Translated by Paul Burns

Notes

1. 'Hunger' and 'malnutrition', like 'underdeveloped country' and 'developing country', are terms that express technically different concepts. But academic formulations tend to use the more euphemistic term for either concept, which is less 'disturbing'.

2. I am relying mainly on his two major works: *Géographie de la faim* (Lyon, 1946), and *Geopolítica de Fome* (São Paolo, 1951).

3. The best source of facts is of course the excellent documentation of the FAO, but I am also referring to prospective studies, particularly those sponsored by the Club of Rome, notably, *Mankind at the Turning-Point*, by Eduard Pestel and Mihajilo Mesarovic.

4. In the line of the 'verstehende Soziologie' propounded by Max Weber.

5. No one has described this experience with more vigour than Elsa Morante in her book, *La Storia. Uno scandalo che dura da diecemila anni* (Turin, 1974).

6. The expression is from Tibor Mende, quoted by René Dumont in, *L'Utopie ou la mort* (Paris, 1974).

7. Cf 'La parole et l'outil', in *Economie en liberté* (Paris, 1975), p. 233.

8. To give some idea of the ecological cost of publicity, each Sunday issue of the *New York Times* consumes between 35 and 50 acres of Canadian forest (From Dumont, *op. cit.*).

9. There is an ample bibliography on mainland China and its achievement, but see especially, Alain Peyrefitte, *Quand la Chine s'éveillera le monde tremblera* (Paris, 2 vols., 1974).

10. Edit. Polyglota Vaticana, 1967, n. 49.

11. Among the outstanding examples of such attitudes on the part of local churches, I would pick out that of the bishops and priests of North-East Brazil, as expressed in their *Ouvi o clamor de meu povo* ('Hear the cry of my poor').

12. *Octogesima Adveniens*, May 1971, n. 41.

13. *Pacem in Terris*, April 1963, n. 159.

Gustavo Gutiérrez

The Poor in the Church

PERHAPS I should make the point at the beginning that the Church is not involved in the question of poverty by the fact that it is present in a poor country. It is involved primarily and fundamentally by the God of the Bible to whom it wants to, and must, be faithful. The fact that the Church is present in a poor country can indeed provide the whole Church with the opportunity better to understand its responsibility to be a community bearing witness to God who himself became poor in Jesus Christ. This leads us to a second point. I have mentioned poor countries but the expression is ambiguous. Strictly speaking I mean countries where the great majority of the population live in poverty caused by an unjust social order. This means that the question of the poor in the Church involves not only the God we believe in but the social conflict we live in.

Bearing this in mind I'd like to suggest some of the thoughts on the problem which have arisen in the course of experiences and discussions during our daily working lives. These lead to the conclusion that the poor today rather than being regarded merely as a 'problem for the Church' raise the question of what 'being the Church' really means.

THE WRETCHED OF THE EARTH

For most of its history, christendom as it was called, the Church has been working out how it sees itself. From within, so to speak. Supernatural salvation is an absolute value of which the Church is the sole guardian. Western Christianity is constructed pastorally and theologically in relation to the believer, the Christian. In order to understand itself the Church looks inwards. This has been called ecclesiocentrism.

11

The historical reasons for this attitude are obvious and easily understandable. When new countries were discovered the task of incorporat-
ing them into the Church was seen as a mission of salvation. The
Church was historically bound up with Western culture, the white race
and the ruling class of European society and its extension throughout
the world was in these western terms. The missionaries followed in the
tracks of the colonialists. Ecclesiocentrism savoured of Westernization.

It is a cliché to say that Vatican II put an end to the 'Christendom'
mentality. The time has come for dialogue and service to the world.
The Church is to turn *outwards* towards the modern world. This world
is hostile to the Church, existed centuries before it, and is proud of its
own values. Pope John XXIII gave the Council the task of opening the
Church to the world, finding an appropriate theological language, and
bearing witness to a Church for the poor. After it had overcome its
initial difficulties, the Church fulfilled the first of these two demands.
The Constitution *The Church in the World* showed the new horizon for
the Church's action seen by Vatican II. It offered an optimistic vision of
the world and its progress, of modern science and technology, the
individual as the subject of history and of freedom, with some reser-
vations about the risks involved in such values. In particular it
affirmed that these values cannot be fulfilled outside the context of the
Christian message. The constitution appealed for collaboration between believers and nonbelievers in 'the just construction of this world
in which they live together'. In this world outside, which should not
however be hostile to the Church, the Lord is present and active and he
also calls the Christian community to greater loyalty to the gospel. In
this world the Church must fulfil its mission as a sign, a universal
sacrament of salvation.

The great claims of the modern world are recognized, but with due
moderation. On the other hand social conflicts are only mentioned in
general terms of the existence of poverty and injustice in the world, and
the necessity for the development of the poor countries. The individ-
ualistic root of bourgeois society is also maintained to a certain extent.
There is no serious criticism of the effects of domination by monopolis-
tic capitalism on the working classes, particularly in the poor countries.
Nor is there any clear realization of the new forms of oppression and
exploitation perpetrated in the name of these modern world values. The
Council is concerned with something else: the time has come for
dialogue between the Church and modern society. That this society is
not homogenous, but divided into conflicting social classes does not
come within the scope of Vatican II. The world to which it is 'opening
up' is bourgeois society.

The third task given by John XXIII to the Council barely appears in its texts. The theme of poverty, 'Schema 14' as it was called in the Council corridors, knocked on the Council's door but only got a glimpse inside. However many Christians have recently been becoming more and more aware that if the Church wants to be faithful to the God of Jesus Christ, it has to rethink itself *from below*, from the position of the poor of this world, the exploited classes, the despised races, the marginal cultures. It must descend into the world's hells and commune with poverty, injustice, the struggles and hopes of the dispossessed because of them is the Kingdom of Heaven. Basically it means the Church living as a Church the way many of its own members live as human beings. Being reborn as a Church means dying to a history of oppression and complicity. Its power to live anew depends on whether it has the courage to die. This is its passover. This sounds like a dream to many people but it is the real challenge confronting the Christian community today. The time will come when any other way of talking by the Church will sound hollow and meaningless. There are now many people working along these lines, in various and perhaps modest ways (the political dimension of the gospel, involvement in the struggle of the poor, defence of human rights, Africanization of the Christian faith, breaking with the colonial past, and so on). The aim is to be faithful to the gospel, and the constant renewal of God's call. Gradually people are realising that in the last resort it is not a question of the Church being poor, but of the poor of this world being the People of God, the disturbing witness to the God who sets free.

SUBVERSION OF HISTORY

Human history is where we encounter the Father of Jesus Christ. And in Jesus Christ we proclaim the Father's love for all human beings. As we have already mentioned, this history is a history of conflict, but we cannot leave it at that. We must also insist that history (in which God reveals himself and we proclaim him) must be *re-read from the viewpoint of the poor*. Human history has been written, as a Brazilian theologian has put it, 'with a white hand', by the ruling classes. The point of view of the 'underdogs' of history is quite other. History must be re-read from this viewpoint of their struggles, resistances and hopes. Great efforts have been made to blot out the memory of the oppressed. This deprives them of a source of energy, historical will and rebellion. Today the humiliated nations are trying to understand their past in order to build their present on solid bases. The history of Christianity has also been written with a white, western, bourgeois hand. We must recall to mind the 'scourged Christs of the Indias', as Bartolomé de las Casas called the Indians of the American continent, and with them all the other poor people who have been victims of the lords of this world. Their memory still lives in cultural expressions, popular religion and the resistance to impositions by the Church bureaucracy. The memory of Christ is present in every hungry, thirsty oppressed and humiliated person, in the despised races and the exploited classes (Cf. Mt. 25). His memory of Christ who 'for freedom has set us free' (Gal. 5:1).

But the phrase 're-reading history' I have used might sound like a mere intellectual exercise if I did not mean it as a *re-making of history*. It is not possible to re-read history unless we enter into the successes and failures of the fight for freedom. Re-making history means subverting it, that is to say 'turning it upside down' and seeing it from below instead of from above. The established order has taught us to think of subversion as something bad, because it threatens it. But contrariwise it is bad to be and perhaps go on being a 'super-versive', supporting the ruling power and seeing history from the standpoint of the great of this world. This subversive history involves a new experience of faith, a new spirituality and a new proclamation of the gospel. Understanding the faith in terms of the historical praxis of liberation leads to the proclamation of the gospel as the very heart of this praxis. This proclamation is a watchguard, an active involvement and solidarity with the interests and struggles of the working classes, the word which becomes effective in action, defines attitudes and is celebrated in thanksgiving.

THE GOSPEL OF THE POOR

The gospel proclaims liberation in Jesus Christ, liberation which uproots all injustice and exploitation and brings friendship and love. I do not mean a liberation which could be interpreted 'spiritually', still so dear to certain Christian circles. Hunger and injustice are not merely economic and social problems but human ones and they challenge the very basis on which we live our Christian faith. As Berdiaer put it, reinterpreting terms frequently used in such circles, 'If I'm hungry it's a material problem, but if someone else is hungry it's a spiritual problem'. Love and sin are historical realities which take place in real situations. That is why the Bible speaks of liberation and justice as opposed to the slavery and humiliation of the poor in history. The *gift of sonship* is accomplished in history. By accepting others as our brothers and sisters we accept this free gift not in word but in deed. This is living the Father's love and bearing witness to it. The proclamation of a God who loves all human beings equally must be embodied in history, become history. Proclaiming this liberating love in a society ruled by injustice and the exploitation of one social class by another, turns this 'becoming history' into an appeal and a conflict. Within a society where social classes conflict we are true to God when we side with the poor, the working classes, the despised races, the marginal cultures. This is the position whence to live and proclaim the gospel. Proclaiming it to the oppressed of this world will show them that their situation is against God's will which is enacted in liberating events. This will help them to realize the vile injustice of their situation.

The gospel read from the point of view of the poor and the exploited, militancy in their struggles for freedom requires a people's Church: a Church which arises from the people, a people who wrest the gospel from the hands of the great ones of this world and thus prevent it being used to justify a situation against the will of the liberating God. When the poor expropriate the gospel from the hands of those who now consider it their private property, we shall have what has recently begun to be called 'the social appropriation of the gospel' in certain popular circles in Latin America. The gospel tells us that the sign of the arrival of the Kingdom is that the poor have the gospel preached to them. It is the poor who hope and believe in Christ, or strictly speaking Christians. Can we turn this round and say that the Christians today are the poor?

Perhaps we should go further and say that the preaching of the gospel will be truly liberating when the poor themselves are the preachers. Then of course the proclamation of the gospel will be a stumbling block, it will be a gospel 'unacceptable to society' and expressed in the vernacular. Thus the Lord will speak to us. Only by listening to this voice will we recognize him as our saviour. This voice speaks 'in ecclesia' with a different tone. Thus the poor of this world are working out their 'historical credo', telling themselves and others why they believe in the Lord who sets free. Because they believe in him in communion with a whole historical past, in the social conditions in which they are living now. In various places many attempts have been made and continue to be made in this direction. It is a mistake to think that Latin America today is totally submerged under repression and fascism. Moreover for the people of the subcontinent, suffering is not something new; it has always been there, but so too have hope and the will to rebel.

For a long time these people have been exiles in their own land, but also making the exodus to regain it. The workers' power of resistance and creativity are incomprehensible to the defenders of the established order, and also disconcerting to those who have recently regarded

themselves as their spokesmen. A few years ago communication between different Christian communities engaged in the struggle for liberation in Latin America was active and enriching. Today the political
and ecclesiastical conditions have changed and the lines have been
broken to a great extent. But everywhere new efforts are starting: for
example, the groups being formed in Brazil. The increasing hunger and
exploitation (especially in the poorer countries), imprisonment (the
political arrests in the whole subcontinent, the bishops who met at
Riobamba) torture and murder (the Honduras peasants, Argentinian
priests) are the price being paid for rebelling against secular oppression
and beginning to understand what the Church and being a Christian
mean today. But these lives and this bloodshed are a radical challenge
to the whole Church, not just the Church in Latin America, requiring
more than mere analysis. Its response to this challenge will decide how
faithful it is to its own authentic tradition and thus to the Lord who
'establishes justice and right'.

How can I sing to God in a foreign land? asked the psalmist in exile.
There can be no Christian life without 'songs' to God, celebrations of
his liberating love. But how can we sing to God in a world full of
oppression and repression? A painful question for the Christian, involv-
ing the whole basis of his faith, requiring something like a new covenant 'with us who are all of us here alive this day' (Deut. 5:3), breaking
the historical covenant made with the ruling culture, race and class. It
requires a covenant with the poor of this world, a new kind of universality. This creates a feeling of panic in some; others lose their old securities,
but many feel a disturbing sense of hope. As José Maria Arguedas puts
it, it is a journey in which 'we feel little knowledge but great hope'.

Translated by Dinah Livingstone

Yorick Spiegel and Klaus Winger

The Tasks of the Church with regard to Psychological Pauperization

RELATIVE poverty in the industrialized countries together with other kinds of deprivation brought about by physical, social and psychological factors have led to another form of penury, characterized above all by social isolation, a lack of relationships and an absence of communication. I propose to discuss here only one aspect of this very complex spectrum: that of the psychological pauperization caused by the alienating structures of the world of work. Paradigmatic relationships in the Federal Republic of Germany today are at present being studied with this problem in mind. I hope therefore that this concrete evidence will enable us to make rather more precise pronouncements about the subject and to draw analogies for other regions and other symptoms of poverty.

THE CONCEPT OF 'PSYCHOLOGICAL PAUPERIZATION'

To understand this concept, we have to go back to the renewed interest in Marxist theory that arose in the Federal Republic in the mid-nineteen-sixties. According to the *Communist Manifesto*, the proletariat had nothing to lose but their chains.[1] Again, according to Marx's *Capital,* 'the accumulation of wealth at one pole also means an accumulation of misery, distress at work, slavery, ignorance, brutalization and moral degradation at the opposite pole, that is, on the side of the class that produces its own product as capital'.[2]

One of the most striking consequences of the economic revival that took place in the Federal Republic from 1945 onwards was a considerable material prosperity. This gave rise to the question as to whether this aspect of Marxist theory had not been made out of date by history.[3] At the same time, however, the counter-argument was put forward that, despite an undeniable improvement in the material conditions of production among wage-earners, there was no halt in the process of pauperization caused by work. All that had really happened was that this occurred at the psychological rather than the physiological level. For the time being at least, material pauperization had been overcome. Psychological pauperization, on the other hand, was becoming more and more pronounced.

Two observations, which do not at first sight appear to be connected, can be made in this context. Firstly, there is public recognition of the frighteningly high proportion and widespread nature of psychological illness in the Federal Republic. Secondly, work which makes severe physical demands has to a great extent been replaced by work making extreme psychological demands.

So far, there are not enough reliable statistics about the extent and the present trend of psychological illness in the Federal Republic. It is so common, however, that it presents a real problem. All physiologists and sociologists active in the world of work agree that the psychological demands made by the organization of work are continuously increasing. This can be observed in three areas: the intensification of psychological demands, the increased intensity of labour and the disqualification that is taking place in administration as a result of the introduction of data processing.

Psychological rather than Physical Demands Made by Work

The model that is commonly applied in this case is that of technological development in three stages. In the case of industrial production in the Federal Republic of Germany, the first of these three phases was production by artisans. This was followed by mass production, in which specialized plant and the conveyor-belt technique were used. We have now entered the third stage of automation in production. This is characterized by use of self-regulating machinery, the worker being the minder and regulator of the process of production.[4] This has led to decisive changes in the conditions of work. Modern places of work require above all supervision, control and guidance. There has been a marked decrease in hard physical labour. The worker has to respond to certain prearranged signals and intervene quickly and directly, exercising control. The structure of the demands made on him has changed from the purely corporeal or physiological to the spiritual, mental and psychological: 'For the assimilation and processing of data determining the course of work, considerable ability to perceive, abstract, react and think logically is required'.[5] At the same time the worker's degree of personal responsibility and, with it, his fear of failure have also increased.[6]

These psychological demands have led to a more widespread occurrence of vegetative breakdowns and psychoneurotic modes of behaviour.[7] 'Direct communication and co-operation become more and more difficult and the uniformity of the pattern of work and its failure to stimulate often cause feelings of fatigue and listlessness, low pulse rate and blood pressure and a reduction in activity and the power to react'.[8]

Increased Intensity of Labour

At the same time, the technological possibilities of the second phase of undertakings have been completely exhausted in order to increase the intensity of work. The scarcity of personnel on the one hand and the economic crises of 1967 and 1974 on the other have led to serious attempts on the part of businesses to lower the greatly increased wages bill by intensifying labour. As a result, a great deal of attention has been given since the mid-nineteen-sixties to the problem of 'scientifically' creating optimum conditions of work and its application. We now have at our disposal a great number of methods which make it possible for labour intensity to be increased. Achievement can be concentrated by the introduction of the two-hand system, the intensification of the process of work and the reduction of complicated work to a mechanical form of work that is concerned with purely physical processes of thought. Movements can be simplified by the creation of simple and habitual processes and the elimination of all superfluous movement. Excessive expenditure of energy can be reduced by a rhythmical style of work and an exact calculation of energy input.[9] It is only when all the possibilities of intensifying labour have been exhausted that the transition to automation is justified.

Disqualification in Administration

In administration, the introduction of electronic data processing has led to a division of the unified activity previously carried out by specialized departmental officials between semi-skilled, machine-oriented workers on the one hand and highly qualified experts on the other. Preliminary and supplementary forms of work that can be done by machines have been taken over by part of the work force of employees and officials. The task of dealing with 'difficult cases', which is an activity that requires much higher qualifications,[10] is carried out by another and much smaller part of the work force. The threat of disqualification has led in the intermediate levels to a fear that professional identity will be lost. It is in the process of socialization that is peculiar to these intermediate levels of employment that values such as self-fulfillment in work, autonomy and professional motivation are strongly emphasized, but the changes that are taking place now make it much more difficult for these professional expectations to be fulfilled. The introduction of electronic data processing has led, if not to unemployment, then to a decisive change, which is felt as a deep breach in the professional career of those concerned. The latter find such changes all the more difficult to bear if 'no subjective orientations and experiences are available to replace these'.[11] There are many indications of the fact that the changes that have taken place in the sphere of work have made it impossible for professional workers to fulfill their self-image so that it will lead to self-respect. The loss of the professional aspects of self-fulfillment, individualization, professional satisfaction and success in work have increased the risk of illness.[12]

Work and the Satisfaction of Human Needs

In the first part of this article, I tried to point out the social phenomena to which the concept of 'psychological pauperization' was related. In this second part, I shall try to indicate the ways in which psychological pressure or stress at the place of work and psychological illness are connected and to illustrate this connection by means of two examples.

For my point of departure, I shall take a socio-medical investigation of patients in a clinic. According to this investigation, which was carried out by J. Siegrist,[13] 90% of the patients questioned were conscious of a connection between psychological pressure in their professional life and their psychosomatic disorders. In the first place, the factors causing stress were seen to be the increased speed of work resulting from rationalization. In the second place, there were outside interventions. In the third place, those questioned spoke of the discrepancy between professional ability and the task in hand (too much and too little demand made). In the fourth place, there was the problem of restriction to tasks that were always the same (for example, secretaries limited to pure shorthand and typewriting). In the fifth place, stress was caused by deficiencies in the organization of labour and, in the sixth place, it was the result, according to those interrogated, of mistakes, over which those concerned had no influence. A foreman in a metalworking firm, for example, declared: 'The worst is the strain on my nerves. On the one hand, I am held responsible and on the other I have not got the necessary authority. There is a contradiction here'.

This investigation may throw light on the effects of changes in the organization of work. A place of work is never an emotionally neutral place in which the worker spends the number of hours that he is required to spend there and receives a suitable wage for this. On the contrary, it is the place to which the worker brings the only commodity that he has to offer: that is, his power to work, and with it his own identity. These he takes as it were to offer them at a market over which he has only very limited control. A decision is made at this market about how much he is worth and what he is capable of doing. He is also subject to the conditions of work and the demands made by it, factors that he can determine himself only to a very limited extent. His power of decision as to whether the work offered will be meaningful and fulfilling for him is also severely limited. Neither the increasing intensity of work nor the lowering of the demands made in many places where automation has been introduced cannot be changed in any way by the individual worker.

Although the conditions of work are largely determined by others and most employees have no influence on this, there are also positive functions connected with the place of work, the full significance of which usually only becomes apparent when these functions are lost. Regular work is associated with various forms of social recognition and security. The place of work is therefore a place of social contacts and relationships and provides the possibility of self-expression. It is possible to do things there that will gain the respect of one's colleagues and one can count on simple expressions of solidarity. Certain loyalties of an emotional nature also develop at the place of work. (There is, for example, a common attitude of loyalty to 'my' firm, which is often exploited by the employer.) Political information is also communicated by the representatives of the employees and a process of socialization often takes place at the centre of work.

Every change in the organization of work which the employees think of as negative produces effects on the background of previous positive experiences which, if they cannot be either assimilated or eliminated, are bound to lead in the long run to various forms of psychological pauperization. The consequences of the intensification of labour, the impoverishment of work, professional disqualification, night and shift work and the loss of place of work are directly traceable both to the process of rationalization and technological development of the competitive individual capitalist economy and to attempts to save costs put into effect by the public sector with a minimum of attention devoted to the labour factor. The further consequence of this is that the employees are expected to bear the brunt of these changes in the sphere of work. Whenever an economic crisis arises, it is thought to be even less necessary to take the labour factor into consideration.

I would now like to show, by means of two examples—firstly, night and shift work and secondly unemployment—how changes in the organization of work affect the psychological health of the employees.

EXAMPLE 1: NIGHT AND SHIFT WORK

Night and shift work is much more widespread than is generally recognized. Even in 1965, 11.2% of those actively employed in the Federal Republic did night work. This percentage includes many officials, especially those employed by the Federal Railways. In transport generally and in the medical and paramedical professions, night work is stagnating. In the sphere of industrial work, on the other hand, it is constantly increasing. From 1965 to 1972, the number of employees doing night work as well as work on Sundays and holidays increased in the Federal Republic from 2.4 to 3.8 million.[14] This means that about 10 million people in the country are involved in shift work, either directly or as members of families.

The reasons for this increase are not difficult to find. Investment costs have risen and with them the capital costs per place of work. This has forced employers in the private sector to keep production going all round the clock. There are few legal sanctions that can be used against this form of labour and little is known about the public effects or the extent of this practice. It has therefore proved possible to employ technological processes that are designed to operate over a twenty-four hour period. Certain public services, such as care of the sick and public transport, are needed, but what very often happens is that a need for such public services is only recognized when night work is introduced as part of the production process. Transport and its control have therefore to be provided by the public sector simply because the legal possibility of night work exists.

The psychological stress of night and shift work is particularly noticeable in the disturbance of the rhythm of day and night experienced by the work. This disturbed rhythm does not change even when night work goes on for several months. This rhythm is not biologically determined. It is due to the fact 'that, in night work, no change can be made in the worker's consciousness of time and of social contacts, the two main factors in determining man's attitude to time. The consequence of this is that every night worker continues to be conscious of what those who do not work at night are doing and what he himself really ought to be doing'.[15] It is, on the other hand, remarkable how quickly the rhythm of day and night is adapted, for example, during a flight, to the different rhythm of day and night in the country to be visited, in other words, to the pattern of life prevailing in the new country.[16]

The worker almost always experiences greater stress when he is obliged to adopt a way of life with changed phases. This is because he has to work at a time when his performance is inevitably at a low ebb, because he is physically and psychologically oriented towards a process of recovering his energy and the majority of people in his environment are also experiencing this need. This greater stress during night work is further increased by the fact that the time the worker spends asleep is considerably abbreviated,[17] because of the higher noise-level during the day and the living conditions at home, which does not provide a space that is insulated from the rest of the family. At the same time, his sleep is of a lower quality.

What has been stressed in general in investigations into family behaviour in the working class can be applied even more emphatically to families involved in shift work.[18] R. Wald has pointed out that, because so little free time is available to the shift worker, that is, time that is not taken up by work, travel, necessary domestic tasks and sleep—it amounts on average to two or three hours—the shift worker's social contacts are almost entirely restricted to his family.[19] In fact, 79% of those questioned by Wald spend their free time in the narrower or wider circle of their family. It is not possible, however, to deceive oneself into thinking that night and shift workers enjoy an intense life of togetherness with their families, in view of the short time of freedom available to them.

According to Wald's survey, contacts outside the family were firmly rejected, often on the basis of the conviction that they usually came to nothing in the end.[20] Wald himself suggested that these contacts were rejected because it was impossible for them to have a permanent value. Most workers even had no contact at all (or hardly any contact) with more than 70% of their colleagues outside the place of work. This, it may be assumed, would also apply to an even greater degree to night and shift workers, who for the most part do not have any opportunity, after finishing a shift at 2:00 pm or 6:00 am, to find a suitable place (public house) to meet.

This means that family life, as a very restricted sphere of social contacts, is always subject to a high degree of psychological pressure. Every event that departs from the routine is a threat to its ability to function properly. Such events would include, for example, difficulties in connection with the family's schooling, outside care of the young children or an attitude on the part of individual members of the family that is not in accordance with these demands, such as the growing need on the part of the wife to express personal emancipation. The family system is frequently on the verge of extreme stress and every departure from the routine is bound to lead to violent arguments and aggressive actions, in an attempt to restore the old routine. 'The limits imposed by the social structure on the possibilities of life open to the working class as a whole and to each individual member of that class have resulted in a daily renunciation of every modest aspiration and a renewed submission to the 'immovable' laws of production, from which it is apparently impossible to escape. These limits to the possibilities of life therefore form the real basis of psychological deprivation in the more seriously exploited sections of the working class.'[21]

EXAMPLE 2: UNEMPLOYMENT

Mass unemployment has become a reality for the Federal Republic. The number of unemployed fluctuates—according to the variations in the trade cycle—at round about a million. This does not take into account the very considerable but not precisely known figure of young unemployed men and unemployed women who have returned to their homes. Mass unemployment has revealed itself as an evil that is inherent to the capitalist economic system as such. It is one of the consequences of a system which makes use of the labour force exclusively within the framework of the profitability of capital investment and disregards the needs that are related to work. Various measures, such as rationalization, technologization, disqualification, the movement of places of work to other towns and the concentration of production, are carried out only on the basis of economic expediency, whereas measures to make work easier are often rejected.[22] The traditional working-class fear of unemployment, which has never disappeared,[23] has re-emerged after many years, during which the proneness of the capitalist system to economic crises had remained hidden behind a growing prosperity. Although this fear is subjective, it is nonetheless very real. The class structure of our society has once again become strikingly apparent in the fate of the individual worker as well as collectively. The ideology of the prosperous society, which is very much in accordance with the dream of the working class, is showing signs of breaking down under the strain of real mass unemployment, a phenomenon which fundamentally threatens the life of every employee.

We have the striking example of the young worker, who has been unemployed for more than six months, but who sets off at six o'clock every morning with his brief-case under his arm and returns home at five o'clock every evening. This points to one of the fundamental aspects of the effects of unemployment on those concerned: that if work, as the basic reality of life, is effectively destroyed, outward appearances have still to be kept up. Why is this?

'The continuity of the individual's social biography is destroyed when he is set free from the process of production. According to one member of the Enka concern, which has recently been hit by unemployment: "A man's life can only have a perspective if it has an underlying certainty of existence. His pattern of living and thinking is based on this existential certainty and this basis has now been destroyed".'[24]

The misery of unemployment has material and psychological effects at the deepest level on the worker's life. The analysis of the problem of shift work has already drawn attention to the central importance of wage-earning activity in giving form and content to the worker's life, his family and social relationships. 'Work', that is, the capacity to work or the required skills, is the only commodity that the wage-earner has to offer on the social market. It therefore forms the centre of his identity. If the ground is taken away from under this identity, there are inevitable consequences for the material and psychological conditions of the worker's existence, which is subject to the dictates of a certain clearly defined middle-class stress on outward appearance and has therefore to be adapted to the middle-class way of life. The contrast between the public, collective form of expending all one's energy at work and recovering privately at home (in the form of the typical middle-class nuclear family) is usually resolved in the case of the modern worker by his identifying his values and forms with these middle-class values and forms. These can be purchased with the results of selling one's labour (which has a ruinous effect on the worker's physical and psychological health). They also form the outward, but emotionally highly charged shell of the worker's identity. If the ground is taken away from under this identity by unemployment and there is no political class-consciousness, in other words, no anti-middle-class, proletarian attitude, on the part of the worker, there will inevitably be problems in all the various spheres of material, social, psychological and other relationships[25] with which the worker has so far been able to identify himself.

If a worker is affected by unemployment, the economic potential of his whole family is considerably diminished. The inevitable result of this is at least a partial withdrawal from those relationships and activities outside the family that call for financial expense. Attempts that have hitherto been made to compensate for the social exclusion of workers and their families by enabling them to acquire certain (lower) middle-class status symbols can, in such circumstances, no longer be carried out completely. If they are continued, they may lead to serious debts.

The most serious restriction of social contacts is to be found in the loss of the relationships with colleagues that went with membership of the firm or place of work, as well as the similar loss of all other forms of public life as a worker, especially those represented by membership of the trade union. (Trade union activities outside work and during free time are very inadequate in the Federal Republic.) A further serious loss is that of contacts connected with the immediate spatial, temporal and personal sphere of the place of work. (These include, for example, the habit of a quick glass of beer after the shift and that of travelling to and from work together.)

A loss of stability of rôles in the private sphere can be added to this loss of social position in contacts at work when unemployment arises. When he is employed, the father's authority is based essentially on his potential to earn; when he is unemployed, however, especially for a long time, this authority is questioned. His function, which is to ensure the existence of the family during employment, becomes a burden during unemployment. His position of power as the one who maintains the family and as a successful model of professional activity is drastically reduced. The relationship between the husband and the wife also changes: the wife, who has tended to be dominated during employment now becomes dominant during the husband's unemployment. (This also applies to the children.) A relationship of interdependence, which had, until the husband's unemployment been the guarantee of cohesion, frequently breaks down and inhibited frustration and suffering often break out in aggression.

Unemployment, then, contains a serious danger for all those involved in it. It threatens to break down the already existing, individually and socially accepted patterns by which reality is defined. This threatened breakdown of forms and values is very serious, because these provide the usual means by which the individual worker can be kept in stability as far as his material existence and his psychological identity are concerned. If it proves impossible for these patterns to be assimilated into other existing social and ideological patterns of action and understanding, present in the organized public life of the workers, then the way is clearly open for psychological pauperization.

EXPLOITATION AND HUMAN NEEDS

Psychological pauperization is a phenomenon affecting the whole of society. It does not simply affect people involved in the process of work or those who have been eliminated from this process by unemployment. Even children and old people can suffer from it. Nonetheless, the two examples discussed above show clearly enough that three conclusions can be drawn.

1. The satisfaction of human needs is to a great extent dependent on the experiences of the individual at and with his place of work.

2. The threat and the reality of psychological pauperization becomes

greater as the organization of work becomes less able to satisfy these needs. This psychological pauperization can take various forms: inability to work, psychosomatic illness, loss of social contact, inability to give a suitable form to life, alcoholism and dependence on drugs and so on.

3. The psychological pauperization of an individual in his work or when he loses his work also has an effect on the members of that individual's family, causing forms of psychological pauperization in the latter as well. Conflicts arising in marriage because of the husband's shift work also frequently cause psychological difficulties in the children.

I do not claim that psychological pauperization is conditioned exclusively by the organization of work within the capitalist system. There are certainly other causes, such as the constant shortage of material resources in the industrial countries, the limitations imposed on time in the human sphere and the fundamental biological condition of man, including the process of aging and forms of socialization in early childhood. All the same, one of the chief causes of pauperization is the organization of work.

In the present phase of highly industrialized capitalism, competition between individual capitalist units is conducted above all on the basis of highly developed technology. Exploitation of the productive labour force no longer takes place on the basis of physical violence. It is done above all on the basis of the plant installed, all of which calls for certain forms of work: for example, the conveyor belt, night work and machine minding. The pace of work can also, for instance, be speeded up as desired, until it reaches the limit imposed by the physical and above all the psychological strain that is expected of the worker and can be borne by him, even if this is at the expense of long-term psychological pauperization.

On the one hand, the plant installed and used by individual capitalist units in their competitive struggle with other units is becoming less and less able to satisfy the variety of needs evoked by the place of work. On the other hand, workers are being more and more completely liberated by the modern plant and exposed at the same time to social isolation with all its psychological consequences. In this rapid process of technological development, automation and data processing, used in the interest of organized capitalism in the private sector, little consideration is given to the individual's needs, which in the past were satisfied by his work.

The point of departure for the capitalist ideology has for a long time been that human needs are best satisfied in competition between individual capitalist units. Goods are produced in the most rational possible way and they are also produced to satisfy individual needs. In this process, however, it has not been taken sufficiently into account that human needs are not simply satisfied by means of goods—they are also satisfied by the organization of work itself. If these human needs cannot be satisfied by the place of work, the purchase of goods can only partially and to a limited extent act as a compensation.

It is, however, becoming more widely recognized that the satisfaction of human needs is brought about to a great extent by the organization of work and for this reason there is a need for a way of thinking about society that concentrates on the place of work and the form that it should take.[26] There is, in other words, a need for work to be humanized by 'adapting the conditions of work to the qualities, needs and interests of the employees'.[27] Consideration must be given to 'the short- and long-term effects of certain demands made on health, professional mobility, the ability to learn and other aspects of social opportunities'.[28] This means that everything that plays an important part in the organization of places of work, the environmental conditions, the hierarchical relationships and even the decisions regarding investment and the installation of plant and new techniques have all to be taken into account. This cannot be done unless firms and enterprises are radically democratized.

THEOLOGY AND PSYCHOLOGICAL PAUPERIZATION

The problem of work is also a theological problem. This was made quite clear by a statement made by a company director, Dr H. A. Bischoff: 'Man is in no sense at the centre of the industry. That place is occupied by economic success . . . Because all means must function, people must also function . . . The industry does not need people as people, whom God called by their names, but as functions . . . Because people are parts of a whole—of the industry—they are replaceable parts and spare parts. Spare parts must be ready to hand. They must be catalogued. They must have a number . . .'[29]

Even if the churches have only very limited opportunities to influence social change, Christians should not sit back in resignation, as though they were impotent to change developments in society and could at the most only do a little to slow down or avert the most pernicious effects. We would suggest an improvement in the existing possibilities and a better organization. This could be done at two levels: 1. at the level of a re-interpretation and further development of the Christian tradition; 2. at the level of the spheres of activity in which the Church is already engaged.

A further development in theological thinking, directed towards a long-term change in values, could take place along the following lines:

1. A great importance is accorded to the family in the Christian tradition. There have been frequent conflicts between the Church and the State over the question of the legal rights of families (the rights of parents, divorce and abortion). Communication in the family has been traditionally regarded in Christianity as important—particularly such aspects as the I-Thou relationship, the mother's sacrifice for her children and the authority of the father. On the other hand, however, theologians have so far done little to evaluate the importance of the sphere of work, apart from attempts in the past to interpret work as service, calling and duty. (This interpretation was firmly oriented towards the capitalist ethic and was predominantly Protestant).[30]

The family has clearly received a rather one-sided emphasis in theology and this may be the reason why theologians have for so long been blind to the dependence of the family on the organization of work. There is no more destructive influence on the functions of the family than night and shift work. Nothing is more certain to undermine the father's authority than unemployment. Yet the churches devote a great deal of propaganda to prevent certain changes from taking place in the law of marriage and are silent about questions which point to the causes of marital breakdown. If theological symbolism is able to preserve man's existence, then man should be able to see himself in the image of God, who is not a being resting in himself, but is active and is also happy to take pleasure in his work and find it good in the rest of the seventh day of his creation, a God who does not have a love-hate relationship with his work.

2. This love-hate relationship which so many workers have with their work shows the extent to which the need for communication and social recognition within and outside the process of industrial work has been ignored. The worker very frequently feels that he is no more than a cog in the machinery of his work-place. His work may not even be meaningful to him. He believes that he could easily be replaced. The monotony of his work or the great stress it imposes on him cause him to suffer. His anonymous employer has cunningly promoted a sense of 'loyalty', so that he is even more deeply hurt when he is suddenly dismissed. These are a few examples of an extreme neglect of human needs in industry that can easily lead to psychological pauperization.

This all points to the fact that any theology of work must clearly take case studies into account. There are many indications in biblical theology of the tedium of work, but it is obviously not possible for biblical theologians to point to cases of exploitation in work or of employees being deprived of what belongs to them. It is clearly outside the competence of the theologian or biblical scholar, whose standpoint is historical, to speak of forms of exploitation in industrial work.

The theologian who is trying to develop a theology of work can therefore not simply present work either as a divinely instituted duty or as a hardship that is contrary to God's will. He has, however, to indicate the forms of exploitation that lead to psychological pauperization. He should not only point to the happiness of family life or to the degree of psychological disturbance underlying the industrial process. The fundamental question in this theology is whether this world is good or evil.

3. In recent centuries, theologians have been at pains to stress the importance of the individual in contrast to the power of society. They have traditionally tried to show that the individual, who is severely tested by society, has, in his individual relationship with God, a place where he can ultimately affirm his own and others' existence. At the same time, however, this emphasis in theology has also led to the religious conviction that suffering in this world has to be assimilated privately. We have already seen in the two main examples discussed above how the worker can easily come to regard loss of work as a personal failure and how his family can accept this evaluation of the situation, even though he is objectively the victim of an economic process over which he has no control. There is also the case of the foreman who has no power to make decisions of this kind, but who is held responsible for mistakes made. In industry, then, competing against rivals in the economic struggle, the individual can easily end by being resigned in his attitude, losing his job, suffering from psychosomatic disorders and even blaming himself for his defeat in this process. What is more, this individual assimilation of suffering at work, encouraged by the theology of the past, can also prevent the development of a suitable political organization of the conflict.

4. Finally, no theology of work would be complete if it did not take into consideration the Christian concept of justice. The problem of the just relationship between performance and reward dominates the sphere of industrial relationships today. There are many forms of psychological pauperization that are connected with the experience of being treated unjustly. Examples of this experience are the rejection of a wage demand, the sense of being treated less well than others, and, in the case of promotion, being passed over for no clear reason. All these experiences lead easily to the conviction that there is no justice in society and the individual therefore becomes resigned and defeated. This sense of justice can also be exploited by the employer. The introduction, for example, of a 'scientific' evaluation of the place of work by

the employer in order to increase production can at the same time give the mistaken impression that this is an attempted re-organization.

Theologians in the past produced a highly developed analysis of the connection between performance and reward, but hardly any work at all has been done in the sphere of concrete problems of justice or injustice in the place of work, despite the fact that the just relationship between work performed and wages received has become a matter of supreme importance today. Because of this problem, which causes so much psychological pauperization, it is important for theological questions to be asked about the part played here by the justice of God.

POSSIBLE CHURCH INITIATIVES

There are five levels at which the Church can take an initiative in this problem of psychological pauperization.

The Church as a Political Lobby

In the Federal Republic, the Church has proved that it has a good deal of potential strength. This emerged particularly in the debate to have the law concerning abortion changed. The Church, then, has considerable influence in Germany in the question of protecting human life (in this case unborn). It might well have become better understood in society if it had taken as its point of departure a theological presentation of the conditions governing a dignified human life. The concrete demands made by the German trade unions for a 'humanization of work'[31] should be taken up by the Church. Not only Sunday shift work, but also the whole phenomenon of exhaustion brought about by the process of work and the loss of social contacts have a negative influence on Church work. Various initiatives have been taken by Church workers to eliminate and control shift work in industry. The Church, however, has never succeeded in acting effectively as a political lobby. There are many institutions run by the Church for old people (particularly homes, clubs and the provision of various services), but the Church has never campaigned for special legislation to deal with the problem of old age, despite the almost unlimited opportunities in this sphere.

Work in the Parishes

The parish structures provide the Church with an apparatus that would make it possible for problems of psychological pauperization to be dealt with in groups. Even though these problems and those affected by them are not strongly represented in churches with mainly middle-class congregations, it would be possible to encourage awareness in such parish groups. It would, however, be necessary to think carefully in advance about how the question should be conveyed to parishes.

Individual Conversations

The theme of psychological pauperization will also occur in individual conversations if the parish priest is ready to listen. Problems related to work often lie behind family and domestic conflicts, even though they are not always openly recognized as such by those seeking counsel. There are many examples of this: anxiety about the place of work, fear of aging, questions of justice, self-identification with the firm, relationships with others at work, anxiety about health and so on. The parish priest may recognize that fatigue at work and the priority of the worker's family may make it difficult or impossible to fulfill religious duties. In that case, he will be ready to listen to what the worker and his family have to say about the anxieties and stresses caused by work. The same also applies to women at work. The times when the nursery or pre-school is open demonstrate the extent to which the church is concerned with the problem of the wife who goes out to work. The nursery is also a useful place of contact between the working wife and the priest.

Public Symbolic Actions

Although the Church should try to point out the direction that can be followed in any long-term changes in attitudes towards work, structures, values and interpretations, it should, of course, never undertake the rôle of a political party. It must, however, point out, by means of public 'symbolic actions', the side on which it stands and indicate its vision and understanding of the fundamental conflicts in society and at work. Any activity undertaken by Christians in the political, democratic sphere should be clearly seen. An example of this kind of symbolic action is the involvement of Christian groups when there is a threat of dismissals and unemployment at a place of work. A concrete example of this involvement was the initiative taken by Catholic and Protestant priests in Speyer when the Volkswagen factory there was threatened with closure.

There are many abuses within Christian parishes themselves. Several of these are connected with the problem of psychological pauperization. Examples are Church homes or institutions where old people, psychologically disturbed patients or young deprived persons have to live together in circumstances that are unsuitable for the inhabitants.

There may, for instance, be insufficient therapy, contacts with the outside world or social activities. If such symbolic actions are not to fail or end disappointingly for all those involved in them, they have to be carefully prepared and evaluated.

Partners and Allies

The Church is not capable of changing the underlying causes of psychological pauperization alone. The churches have to work together and with other bodies if such a widespread phenomenon as psychological pauperization is to be understood and dealt with. The churches need allies and partners. The trade unions are well qualified to fill this rôle, because they have access to the causes of psychological pauperization and, in Federal Germany at least, have played a large part in assessing and organizing places of work and studying unemployment and its problems as well as the question of the humanization of work. There are also many spheres here, as there are in every organization, where the everyday routine of the personnel is not even noticed or else lies outside the interest of the organizers.

CONCLUSION

Re-organization of work and the intensification of labour, disqualification of professional staff, night and shift work and unemployment can all lead to a loss of psycho-social self-fulfilment and stability. Since this threat to the worker's identity can usually only be assimilated individually, this privatization frequently leads to the destruction of norms and values, psychological decompensation and increased psychological pauperization. This re-organization of work, which brings so much misery in its wake, is, however, not the cause of technical compulsions, but the result of the processes of technological advance and rationalization which are carried out by competing members of the private sector (and the public sector) at the cost of the well-being of the workers and without regard to the fulfilment of the workers' needs that should be satisfied at the place of work.

Psychological pauperization also has an effect on all the activities undertaken by the churches. This is apparent whenever the churches speak about the 'idleness', passivity and isolation of modern man. It is, after all, not easy to preach to people who are psychologically broken. The churches have to learn to what a great extent the psycho-social identity of the workers is won and lost at the place of work. They have also to learn how best to relate the Christian theological symbols of the active God, the fall, divine salvation and God's justice to the situation of active man today—a situation of exploitation, performance and reward and organized labour. Finally, all Christians have to learn not to become passively resigned in the face of their task to change the world. They have to carry out this task, but not alone. They need the active co-operation of those who have already taken up the cudgels against psychological pauperization.

Translated by David Smith

Notes

1. K. Marx and F. Engels, *Manifesto of the Communist Party*.

2. K. Marx, *Das Kapital*, I, p. 674 ff.

3. See, for example, W. Wagner, *Verelendungstheorie. Die hilflose Kapitalismuskritik* (Frankfurt, 1976).

4. H. Kern and M. Schumann, *Industriearbeit und Arbeiterbewusstsein*, I (Frankfurt, 1970), p. 27 ff.

5. *Sieben Berichte, Wirtschaftliche und Soziale Aspekte des technischen Wandels in der Bundesrepublik Deutschland*, 1, *Kurzfassung der Ergebnisse* (Frankfurt, 1970), pp. 226 ff.

6. W. Bungard and H. E. Lück, 'Arbeit in sozialer Isolation', in *Arbeit und Leistung*, 1971, pp. 189–91.

7. H. Valentin and others, *Arbeitsmedizin* (Stuttgart, 1971), p. 9.

8. H.-U. Deppe, *Industriearbeit und Medizin* (Frankfurt, 1973), p. 125; A. Gubser, *Monotonie im Industriebetrieb* (Berne & Stuttgart, 1968), pp. 79 ff.

9. *Industriearbeit und Gesundheitsverschleiss* (Frankfurt, 1974), Exkurs: 'Wichtige Lohnfindungsmethoden', pp. 80–4.

10. N. Altmann and others, *Öffentliche Verwaltung* (Frankfurt, 1971), p. 13.

11. F. Böhle and N. Altmann, *Industrielle Arbeit und soziale Sicherheit* (Frankfurt, 1972), p. 41.

12. C. Rebell, *Sozialpsychiatrie in der Industriegesellschaft* (Frankfurt, 1976), p. 91.

13. J. Siegrist, 'Belastungen der Arbeitssituation bei Angestellten', in *Zeitschrift für Allgemeinmedizin, Der Landarzt*, 42 (1971), pp. 1037 ff.

14. *Materialien zur Lebens- und Arbeitssituation der Industriearbeiter in der BDR* (Frankfurt, 1973), tab. 64.

15. J. Rutenfranz, 'Arbeitsphysiologische Aspekte der Nacht- und Schichtarbeit,' *Arbeitsmedizin, Sozialmedizin, Arbeitshygiene*, 1967, pp. 17–73.

16. H.-U. Deppe, *op. cit.*, p. 128.

17. J. Rutenfranz, *op. cit.*, p. 17; see also W. Menzel, *Menschliche Tag-Nacht-Rhythmik und Schichtarbeit* (Basle, 1962), pp. 134–41.

18. J. Miehe, 'Schichtarbeit', in K. Thomas, *Analyse der Arbeit* (Stuttgart, 1963), pp. 251–64.

19. R. Wald, *Industriearbeiter privat* (Stuttgart, 1966), p. 54; J. Miehe, 'Schichtarbeit', *op. cit.*, p. 43.

20. R. Wald, *op. cit.*, pp. 34, 72.

21. K. Winger, *Determinanten der Sozialisation in Schichtarbeiter-familien. Materialien zur kritischen Analyse von Devianztheorien*, Manuscript (Marburg, 1974).

22. See J. Hoffman and W. Semmler, 'Kapitalistische Krise und Arbeitslosigkeit in der Bundesrepublik,' *Probleme des Klassenkampfs* 5 (Dec. 1972), pp. 125 ff.

23. O. Negt, *Soziologische Phantasie und exemplarisches Lernen* (Frankfurt & Cologne, 1972), pp. 45 ff.

24. G. Paul and A. Wacker, 'Psychologische Erfahrungsdimensionen der Arbeitslosigkeit', *Politikon, Göttinger Studentenzeitschrift*, 75 (April 1975), p. 15.

25. See, for example, R. Reiche, 'Proletarische Familie', *Diskus, Frankfurter Studentenzeitung* (June 1973).

26. H. O. Vetter, ed., *Humanisierung der Arbeit als gesellschafts-politische und gewerkschaftlich Aufgabe* (Frankfurt, 1974); M. Helfert, 'Ziele und Durchsetzung der Humanisierung der Arbeit, ' *WSI-Mitteilungen, Zeitschrift des Wirtschafts- und Sozialwissenschaftlichen Instituts des Deutschen Gewerkschaftsbundes*, 28 (1975), pp. 245–56; M. Kittner, 'Mitbestimmung der Arbeitnehmer über die Arbeitsorganisation und über die Ausgestaltung und Umgebung des Arbeitsplatzes', *ibid.*, pp. 256–69.

27. M. Helfert, *op. cit.*, p. 246.

28. *Ibid.*, p. 247.

29. Quotation from *Industriearbeit und Gesundheitsverschleiss, op. cit.*, p. 77.

30. See Y. Spiegel, 'Arbeit und Leistung als sozialethisches Problem', *Wissenschaft und Praxis in Kirche und Gesellschaft*, 65 (1976), pp. 240–56.

31. See the books and articles listed under note 26. See also the theses of the Confédération générale du Travail (CGT), 'Zur Humanisierung der Arbeitswelt', Special edition of *CGT-Informationen* 16 (November 1974), which contains many clear statements about shift work (pp. 16 ff).

Aquinata Böckmann

What Does the New Testament Say about the Church's Attitude to the Poor?

THE New Testament is too far removed from us in time to be able to give us any precise directives in respect of this problem. But it can supply us the models, basic impulses and general advice relevant to today. So long as we ask ourselves: 'What did this or that command of Christ mean in his time?', it is relatively simple. The difficulties begin when we try to establish the relevance of these commands today. We must pay much closer attention to the problems of hermeneutics.[1] But even so we shall still see the thoughts clothed in contemporary terms, and we must have the courage to translate these basic impulses into forms relevant to today. And these forms are continually changing; tomorrow they will be different from today, and in the western world they differ from those in the countries of the Third World. The questions we ask ourselves today are not those of the New Testament, and it is asking too much of the texts to seek answers to concrete problems such as world economy, development aid, freedom from alienation and structural changes directly in the New Testament.

This article does not purport to be an enquiry into the impulses of the New Testament as a whole, hence the reader should not expect a complete exegetical exposition. Nor is it possible to develop the theme taking account of the different layers of tradition. The following considerations are, however, based on the exegetical approach focusing on the gospels, the context of the Judaeo-Christian communities and the Letters of St Paul.

JESUS AND THE CIRCLE OF DISCIPLES IN RELATION TO THE POOR

The Text of the Beatitudes (Lk. 6:20–26; Mt. 5:3–12)

What is the fundamental message and meaning of the beatitudes? The earliest formulation is probably that found in the first beatitude according to Luke where the poor are addressed in the second person without the addition of the words 'in spirit', and with the promise of the Kingdom of God right now. It is to be assumed that this call to salvation dates from the beginning of Jesus' public life (cf. Jesus' programmatic declaration: Lk. 4:18). Jesus addresses himself directly to the poor and awards them the Kingdom of God. In a special way, the *basileia* is intended precisely for the poor. In the original situation those who came to listen to Jesus were presumably simple people from Galilee, in need of salvation, lacking something, and hence seeking out an unknown prophet.

The audience Christ addressed was rooted in the tradition of the Old Testament and knew the prophecies of a Messiah of the poor (cf. Is. 61:1; 58:6). Throughout the Old Testament one can trace the idea that the poor and oppressed may call God their own particular support (cf. among others Is. 25:4; Ps. 69:34; 72:4). In promising the kingdom of God to the poor Jesus reveals that in him the God of the poor has come. They are blessed, not because they are poor, but because Jesus has come expressly for them and hence transforms their poverty. Jesus does not ask for particular conditions or merits. The kingdom of God is not first and foremost a reward for virtue. It is a gift. In doing this Jesus reverses the normal human system of values. The poor take precedence over the rich, the insignificant over the powerful. The Beatitudes can be compared with the Magnificat, which celebrates the reversal of values at the moment of salvation, taking up the Old Testament scheme of humiliation and elevation (cf. Lk. 1:52 f).

If we turn to Luke's version we notice that it is the disciples who are addressed (6:20), i.e. those whom he regards as the Christians of his time. He speaks without alluding to the moral qualities of the poor, the hungry, the weeping and the pursued. These facts apply to the communities of Luke.[2] Luke also knows that following the coming of the Messiah the situation has only been reversed in a few cases. Fulfilment, happiness, reward will only be fully realized in the eschatological kingdom of God, not in the present. The beatitudes must be seen as a consolation for the Christian community. The present aeon is characterized by poverty, oppression and persecution. But some time the situation will be reversed.

In addition to the beatitudes Luke includes four warnings (6:24–26). Again, it is strange that he does not base these warnings on the bad habits of the rich, but merely on the fact of being rich, or full, or laughing or praised. He sees it in terms of very simple polarities. On the one hand, the poor, the hungry and the persecuted; on the other, the rich, the full and the persecutors. Corruption seems to be inseparable from wealth (cf. Lk. 16:9–11). This is also demonstrated in the parables of the rich spendthrift and poor Lazarus (Lk. 16:19–31) and in that of the rich corn farmer (Lk. 12:16–21). Such hard words are found only in Luke who probably had a special experience of the disastrous consequences of wealth. The kingdom of God cannot enter into the rich. Their wealth separates them from the poor whom they no longer see; they amass possessions in this world instead of gathering treasures with God, for example by giving alms (Lk. 12:15–21). Luke's Gospel in particular contains many urgent warnings against wealth (cf. 12:33; 14:33; 16:12). The only legitimate application of wealth seems to be to use it for charitable purposes (Lk. 16:12; 12:33; 11:41).[3]

In Matthew's account the circle of those addressed is extended to include all Christians and all who wish to be. The poor are the humble, the merciful, the just, and so on. In so doing Matthew is upholding the pious poverty of the Old Testament. His injunctions amount to paraphrases of everything embraced by the new justice of the Sermon on the Mount.[4] In keeping with Hebraic thought, poverty and humility are synonymous,[5] hence a purely spiritual poverty without this material basis is virtually inconceivable. The poor in spirit are in need of help, but they accept their situation before God and are prepared to suffer persecution, to hunger for the justice of God. They place their trust in God, they practice charity and they aim for peace. Poverty in spirit becomes an ideal to be strived for by all Christians.

The judgment speech (Mt. 25:31–46) describes these merciful, upright people who give food to the hungry, drink to the thirsty, clothe the naked and visit the sick and the imprisoned. If we compare this with the beatitudes it becomes clear that only those who themselves are truly poor can give this kind of help. And in doing this to one's fellow men, one is doing it to Christ.

Jesus and the Poor

Taken as a whole, the gospel evidence indicates how Jesus always gives preference to those in need of help. Above all, to those who need help in the sense of healing or a cure. According to Luke, Jesus speaks the beatitude of the poor when surrounded by a large crowd of people 'who came to hear him and to be healed of their diseases' (Lk. 6:18). And the connection between healing and preaching the word of God to the poor is also the distinctive mark of John the Baptist (Lk. 7:21f, par Mt. 11:4 f). It is not only a verbal promise of healing, but simultaneously an act of healing. 'Those who are well have no need of a physician, but those who are sick' (Mk. 2:17). Jesus is concerned with healing the whole man. By focusing his attention on the poor and sick and by seeking their company he also gives them a new significance. He himself comes from a simple background and, especially in Galilee, he usually mixes with simple people. He does not consider a person's rank or social class as relevant. He only sees the individual person and how much that person needs him. He dines with the Pharisees and with tax collectors (cf. Lk. 7:36–50; 19:1–10); he is receptive to Nicodemus (Jn. 3:1–21), and is befriended by Lazarus (Jn. 11,3).

Jesus invites children to come to him and sets them up as examples (Mk. 10:13–16 par) and he glorifies infants and small children (Lk 10:21, par; Mt. 11:25). This is also connected with the paradox of giving precedence to the 'last' (Mk. 10:31 par; Mt. 20:16; Lk. 13:30). Jesus even addresses the heathen (Mt. 8:5–13; 21:31f; 15:21–28 par), speaks to the Samaritan woman (Jn. 4:1–42) and sets up the Samaritan as a model (Lk. 10,30–37). He allows a woman sinner to annoint him with precious ointment (Lk. 7:36–50), he forgives the adultress (Jn. 8:1–11), he points out a poor widow as an example to his disciples (Lk. 21:1–4 par), and many women served him (Lk. 8:1–3).

Such actions of Jesus are seen by some as deliberately subversive.[6] Moltmann writes: 'The love of God and the humanity of Christ are biassed towards the wretched and oppressed, the humiliated and the wronged . . . Only through this partisan dialectic does the crucified Christ achieve universal significance.'[7] Jesus takes sides with the poor and, as Rollet points out: 'To claim to side with the poor without changing the conditions which give rise to poverty, i.e. exploitation in the economic, political and cultural spheres, amounts to fraudulence and hypocrisy.'[8] In contrast, Gutierrez describes all such actions of Christ as liberating and political.[9]

On the other hand, there is considerable evidence to prove that Jesus was not a social revolutionary. For example, his open approach towards all political and economic factions. Certain evidence would seem to suggest that he was a member of the zealot party (e.g. proclamation of the kingdom of God, the command to spread the word, his critical attitude towards Herod, the irony in Lk. 22:25, the order to carry a sword in Lk. 22:36, the entry into Jerusalem, and the proof of death).[10] This is, however, opposed by a whole series of other factors which prove that Jesus did not belong to any political party (e.g. the emphasis on using non-violent means, the love of the enemy, the beatification of the peacemaker, the directive to go unarmed on missionary journeys, to remain faithful to the law, and to avoid any political activity).[11] He is severely critical of the social injustices of his day, in particular the difference between rich and poor, which is against the will of God. But nowhere does he call for revolution, nor does he set out a revolutionary programme. God will judge. Jesus exhorts the individual to be self-critical and reflective, to be truly converted and to love his neighbour.[12] He himself wishes to serve, not to rule, and is prepared to undergo death.

The Circle of Disciples and the Poor

Jesus chooses most of his disciples from among the simple people; and there is also a tax collector among them. But one cannot claim, as Belo has done,[13] that they were all members of the proletariat. Judas was presumably a zealot, but it could well be that he betrayed Jesus precisely because the latter was not zealous enough for his liking.

On the whole Jesus demands of his disciples that they relinquish their worldly possessions and follow him, living from one day to the next on alms and the hospitality of the people. The old system of values no longer applies in the circle of the disciples. Instead, they have a communal fund which is apparently intended to cover both living costs and almsgiving (cf. Jn. 13:29; 12:6). Jesus sends his disciples out empty-handed, presumably to ensure that they will not be received by the rich and powerful, but by the small and insignificant. In other words, by those who truly seek salvation.

Jesus commands the disciples to receive the poor into their community (Lk. 14:12f,21). He instils in them the importance of almsgiving in keeping with the piety of the Old Testament. (Lk. 12:33; 6:30–34). Poverty was an accepted factor of life at that time: 'For you always have the poor with you' (Mk. 14:7; Mt. 26:11; Jn. 12:8). The idea of overcoming the causes of poverty could not possibly arise then.

To sum up, we may outline the basic impulses as follows: Priority is given to those in greatest need. And among these we can establish Jesus' preference for the truly poor, the sick, the rejected and the wronged. The decisive factor is not that the person should belong to any specific social group, but that he should be in need of help. Jesus is never fanatical. On the contrary, he is open to all.

The gospels take a critical stance towards social injustice and warn expressly against the dangers of wealth. The best use of wealth is to employ it in doing good for the poor. The necessary prerequisite for true compassion is the attitude of poverty as described by Matthew in the beatitudes. The act of charity towards the least of the brethren is the decisive factor for entry into the kingdom of God. According to the Synoptics, poverty, distress and persecution belong to this world and will only be finally eliminated at the end of time. Unlike today, the causes of this poverty were never called into question.

THE JUDEO/CHRISTIAN CHURCHES

The First Church in Jerusalem according to Acts

In one of the two collective reports describing the life of the first Christians we read: 'There was not a needy person among them' (Acts 4:34). Hence in this church the Old Testament prophecy of Deut. 15:4 is fulfilled. In the people of God everyone should have the basic necessities, and should help one another so that no one goes in need. The early Christian Church symbolizes the new messianic people of God in its perfect form. Christians shared everything or placed their belongings at the disposal of others. (The various reports are contradictory; cf. 2:44; 4:32 b c with 2:45; 4:34 f). And this practical approach in everyday life is a consequence of the celebration of breaking bread. In some texts the following words are added to Acts 4:32: 'There was no difference separating them'. The legitimate claim on possessions becomes a relative one within the brotherhood in Christ, and is transformed into a bond of brotherliness and unity.

In Acts 6:1–6 we read that the apostles combined preaching the word with daily service at table. Later on men are 'full of the Spirit and of wisdom' (Acts 6:3) and are appointed to this duty after prayer and the laying on of hands (6:6)—a sign of the significance of this duty in the early Church (probably thought of in general terms as caring for the needy members of the community[14]).

The Letter of James

The author reprimands his church severely, as described in James 2:1–3, for discriminating between the rich and the poor man, showing the latter to a lesser place. 'Love of the poor and the singling out of the rich are not compatible.[15] The same letter contains a stern warning to the rich (5:1–3) and censures them for exploiting the poor (5:4 6). But this is not followed by a call to rebellion. On the contrary, they are exhorted to wait patiently for the coming of the Lord, which is near at hand (5:10). God will take the deprived into his care. Because the coming of the Lord is thought to be imminent, the question does not arise as to how a better social order might be achieved.

On the basis of this evidence concerning the Judeo-Christian churches the following basic impulses may be discerned: Among the people of God none should go in need. Within the Christian community all are equal; social status is irrelevant. All possessions should be shared or placed at the disposal of others. Care of the needy members of the community is also regarded as extremely important.

The exploitation of the poor by the rich is openly attacked.

PAUL AND THE POOR

The Poor in the Corinthian Church

According to Paul, God has chosen the foolish, those of lowly birth, the despised, even 'things that are not' (1 Cor. 1:26–29). He sees theological significance in the fact that the Church draws its membership largely from the lower social orders. He sees this as the free choice of divine mercy (cf. 1 Cor. 1:18–25) connected with the paradox of the cross, in which God's power and majesty reveal themselves in human powerlessness and humility. The powerless and the humble will find it easier to recognize God through signs of weakness, foolishness and the cross. By electing the weak in this way, values are reversed. The humble are elevated, and the elevated are humbled. All human marks of distinction are superseded. There are some (but not many: 1:26) wise and powerful in the community. But God brings all men together round the elevated Lord in the *koinonia* of the eucharistic celebration. In 1 Cor. 11:17–34 Paul criticizes the behaviour of the Corinthians. The celebration of the eucharist itself is intact; but he objects to the fact that social differences are manifested in the agape that precedes it, when some have enough to eat while others must hunger. He accuses them harshly: 'Do you despise the church of God and humiliate those who have nothing? (1 Cor. 11:22). To allow social differences to arise is to eat unworthily of the Lord's Supper. Each goes ahead with his own meal. Eating and drinking are thus the cause and symbol of division, when they should create and bear witness to unity. If Christians construct social barriers among themselves they cannot bear witness to Christ's act of love, in which he creates unity among men through his own body. Sharing with the poor is the basic prerequisite for the orthodox celebration of the Lord's supper.[16] 'The bread that we break, is it not a participation in the body of Christ? Because there is *one* bread, we who are many are *one* body, for we all partake of the *one* bread' (1 Cor. 10:16 f). The love we receive must flow out towards our fellow men, especially in the form of caring for those in need. Hence a new system of values is instituted. 'There is neither Jew nor Greek, there is neither slave nor free, there is neither male nor female; for you are all one in Jesus Christ' (Gal. 3:28; cf. 1 Cor. 7:22; 12:13). The rich have no precedence over the poor. On the contrary, privilege is to be accorded to the poor. In this way a new order is created within the community of the Church.

Paul and Manual Labour

Some writers have claimed that Paul is the first worker-priest.[17] But he was not really concerned to participate in the workers' (or rather, labourers') world of his day through work. Manual labour does not form a part of his apostolic task. For one thing, he wants to give an example to the negligent; and for another he needs independence in order to carry out his apostolate. His aim is to protect the gospel message from reproach (cf. 2 Thess. 3:7–9); cf. Acts 20:33–35). It must be shown to be trustworthy. By preaching the word freely salvation has the appearance of an unearned gift (cf. however the acceptance of assistance when it is not detrimental to credibility: Phil. 4:10–18).

Koinonia among the Various Churches

Paul refers to the members of the Church in Jerusalem as 'poor' (Rom. 15,26; cf. Gal. 2,10). It is not possible to ascertain whether this was a kind of honorary title along the lines of the Jewish piety of poverty,[18] or whether the community was in fact materially poor (cf. Acts 11:28–30). Paul's letter is more than just a charitable act of assistance; it is a sign of the *koinonia* between the mother Church and its subsidiary branches. The individual churches are united in Christ and have a responsibility towards each other. And this same unity and equality should exist in the 'worldwide' *koinonia* (2 Cor. 8:13 f). Paul says explicitly that this does not mean that the Corinthians should reduce themselves to poverty, but that one community's material abundance should balance out the want of another. And this act of giving and sharing is in no way one-sided, for the Corinthians in their turn benefit from the spiritual abundance of the Church in Jerusalem (2 Cor. 8:14). The same principle of sharing, in fact, as that practised within each local church community. Enriched by Christ's act of love they should freely feel the inner need to help others in their poverty, to assist them materially, to strive for exchange and equality, while being aware that repayment will necessarily be in a different form.

The poor and the slaves outside the Christian community are not taken into consideration in Paul's letters. He does not really develop the idea that Christians should endeavour to create a more just social order. This is presumably due to the fact that Christians form a minority recruited mostly from the lower social orders, and to the fact that the end of the world is expected at any moment. They are as yet not concerned with the structure of this world (cf. 1 Cor 7:29–31). Love within the Christian community is of primary importance here, in the same way that brotherly love figures strongly in the writings of John. This is understandable when one considers that the Church consists of a disparate crowd of people brought together by their love of Christ who discover that they are now brothers in Christ and must acknowledge the consequences of God's love for them.

The main conclusions to be drawn from these points are:
In the Christian community there should be no distinctions of class or rank, for all have been united together by the Lord's supper.
Following the example of Christ's act of love towards mankind, Christians should pass on to others the love they have received, especially by caring for those in need, and by striving to create equality between all men.
The *koinonia* of both spiritual and material riches should also extend beyond the limits of the local church into a universal exchange of mutual giving and taking.

On examining the evidence of the New Testament as a whole, the following factors are given special prominence:
—the precedence of those in need; in particular, the privileges of the materially poor,
—the unity in Christ as a consequence of the Lord's supper which permits no barriers of wealth, status, etc.,
—the warning to the rich; the admonition to share their wealth, to be just and to use their wealth in the spirit of brotherly love.
An attitude of poverty is essential to this code of behaviour.

If these impulses are to be relevant to today, they must be translated into very practical terms. For example, the intercession in the cause of the poor, prophetic warnings to the wealthy, the elimination of poverty, development aid, assistance towards complete liberation, and the active desire for just social structures.
But in doing this, the intentions of Jesus should always be vitally present; the will to serve, to maintain one's own attitude of poverty, to suffer injustice if necessary, and to approach all people openly and without prejudice. And we should certainly not limit our spirit of love merely to the poor within the Christian churches. On the contrary,

conscious of God's universal love for us, we should identify with anyone who is poor, regardless of their creed or religion.

Translated by Sarah Twohig

Notes

1. Cf. H. Schürmann, 'Haben die paulinischen Wertungen und Weisungen Modellcharakter?,'. *Gregorianum* 56 (1975), pp. 237–71; 'L'Impact des normes morales du Nouveau Testament sur la vie chrétienne', *La Documentation catholique* 57 (1975), pp. 761–66.

2. Cf. J. Dupont, *'Introduction aux Béatitudes,' Nouv. Rev. th.* 108 (1976), p. 107.

3. Cf. H.-J. Degenhardt, *Lukas-Evangelist der Armen* (Stuttgart, 1965).

4. Cf. J. Dupont, *Les Béatitudes,* vol. III, (Paris, 1973), pp. 304 f.

5. Cf. *ibid.* pp. 469–71.

6. Cf. F. Belo, *Lecture matérialiste de l'évangile de Marc* (Paris, 1974), p. 262.

7. *The Crucified God* (London & New York, 1974), pp. 76 f.

8. *Libération sociale et salut chrétien* (Paris, 1974), p. 178.

9. *Teologia de la liberacion* (Salamanca, 1972), p. 239; cf. p. 308.

10. Cf. O. Cullmann, *Jesus et les révolutionnaires de son temps* (Neuchâtel, 1970), p. 17.

11. Cf. *ibid.,* pp. 17, 36.

12. Cf. *ibid.,* p. 39–43, 20; cf. M. Hengel, *Was Jesus a Revolutionist?* (Philadelphia), 1971, p. 28; cf. pp. 20–27 *(War Jesus ein Revolutionär?,* Stuttgart, 1970).

13. *Op. cit.,* p. 343.

14. Cf. G. Stähiin, *Die Apostelgeschichte,* (Göttingen, 1970), p. 98.

15. F. Mussner, *Der Jakobusbrief* (Freiburg, 1964), p. 123.

16. Cf. P. Neuenzeit, *Das Herrenmahl* (Munich, 1960), p. 234.

17. E.g, P. Gauthier, *Ich habe Dich gerufen* (Graz, 1969), p. 223 *(Aux prétres, aux réligieuses, aux laics).*

18. Cf. P. Seidenstricker, *Saint Paul et la pauvreté: La pauvreté évangèlique* (Paris, 1971), p. 104.

Michel Mollat

Poverty and the Service of the Poor in the History of the Church

THE historian describes what has happened. He claims no authority to make judgments. Like everything to do with poverty, the relationship of the Church with the poor is filled with ambiguity and contradiction. The fundamental principle, at least, is unequivocal: Christ himself defined the mission to preach the good news to the poor. So the initiative must be taken to go to the poor, and it is a service. Taken together with Christ's description of the works of mercy, the service of the poor becomes a duty of liberation; and, most paradoxical of all, as the tradition of history also notes, helping the poor, liberating them from suffering and oppression is helping and liberating Christ, whose image they are. Thus, though elevated by the Incarnation, the condition of the poor is still an affliction and a trial.

On the other hand, the mission to teach the Beatitudes obliges the Church to eulogize poverty. Not just to eulogize the poor man who accepts his poverty, but to eulogize that poverty directly in itself, as the royal road to salvation. Clearly this eulogy on the plane of spirituality is on a different level from performing the works of mercy, and the apparent contradiction is not insoluble. However, those sent out to preach the Good News were advised to set off without any ties, without any *impedimenta,* in other words taking no luggage—no change of clothes or shoes—without even considering their families. How is one to reconcile two such opposing ideas of poverty?

In fact, there is poverty and poverty; it must always be seen in relation to the historical situation. Whom do we describe as poor? What kind of poverty are we eulogizing? When we talk of voluntary poverty, what do we mean by it? Where does it begin and end? What rules govern it?

The Church's mission being what it is, and the problem such a complex interweaving of the spiritual and physical, the most outstanding paradox would be if the Church, made up of fallible human beings, had fulfilled that mission with utter fidelity. But similarly, it would have been a sign of weakness in the Church, had she been exempt from criticism and protest intended, if sometimes wrongheadedly, to set her back on the right path.

How has the Church confronted two apparently opposing problems? We can look to history for an explanation. Significant events can be found in every period and every place. The experience of a thousand years of medieval Christendom gives plenty of scope for comparison with what has happened in the centuries since then.

Though movements of poverty are quite a different thing from the service of the poor, the historian cannot view them separately. They are of a piece. However, whereas the service of the poor is something continuous, varying only in the forms it takes, movements of poverty are temporary impulses of longer or shorter duration, stimulated either by a fresh enthusiasm for voluntary poverty as asceticism or a spiritual good, by indignation at seeing the poor treated without charity or justice, or by the new problems created by increasing destitution. Whatever their origin, all movements of poverty represent some sort of call to order, a call for a return to the gospel sources. There is, thus, between the service of the poor and movements of poverty a dialectical relationship between a static practice and a dynamic action. This relationship changes with the movement of history, taking its shape to some extent from it; conversely, it contributes to colouring the social complexion of every period. It is important to define some of these words. 'Poor' can have a very wide meaning. A poor man can mean someone so destitute that he has to beg, but could also be someone who, for various reasons, cannot get along without help. His situation may be due to precariousness or lack of financial resources, to being without the food, clothing or lodging needed for survival, to physical or mental handicaps, to loss of liberty, to lack of education, or to having no satisfying human contacts. No one person will be subject to all these deprivations at once, least of all a person who has chosen voluntary poverty. Voluntary poverty may be that of an individual or a community; it may be both at once. Finally, is must be noted also that, relative to different situations and times, the word 'Church' may be used either in the institutional sense of an ecclesial society, in the narrower sense of the ecclesiastical hierarchy who govern the Church, or in the widest sense of the community of the faithful.

If we want to examine a period in the Middle Ages when movements of poverty and the service of the poor both manifested an equal vitality, we must look to the end of the eleventh century and follow developments up to the mid-fourteenth century. To describe the period before the eleventh century, the word that most readily springs to mind is 'sluggish': in fact that would be an unfair exaggeration, but the lot of the poor changed little in an essentially rural society that was slowly developing towards the stability of a hierarchical system of vertical dependence-relationships. The ideal structure of order was taken to be a pyramid of 'orders' whose tranquillity would ensure peace. One could describe it as a social rather than a political Augustinism (though its authenticity as Augustinism remains to be proved).

During those five hundred years, the Church, hierarchy and faithful, never forgot the gospel recommendations concerning poverty and the poor. From the sixth century to the eighth, the poor man was the traditional model of the half-starved creature, the beggar, the victim of the exactions of officials and the calamities of civil wars: this is the picture painted by Gregory of Tours in his *History of the Franks*. There were also the impoverished serfs of Provence and the artisans of Arles, whose archbishop, St. Caesarius preached to them in direct and practical style; he gave the poor help of a different kind by freeing prisoners from the Goths. In Rome, Pope Gregory the Great assisted victims of plague and famine. One can trace a persisting tradition of service of the poor, based on the teaching of the Latin Fathers—especially St Ambrose— and going back to the Greek Fathers: for though the West was gradually forgetting its debt to them, the tirades of such men as John Chrysostom, Gregory of Nyssa and Gregory Nazianzen against the authorities of city and empire had been bitter indeed. An infrastructure of service was then set up with the help of the bishops and with alms from the faithful. In the parishes, the registers represented an assistance fund for all whose names were inscribed in them; at diocesan level, the *Domus Dei* near the bishop's house was the ancestor of the hospital in many a cathedral town today. The last resort of the desperate against oppression and the denial of justice was an 'evangelical denunciation' to the bishop, and the right of sanctuary without respect of persons. The bishop was the 'defender of the poor', just as the goods of the Church were the 'patrimony of the poor' to whom, canonically, a quarter of all tithes were to be given. The high Middle Ages which were the period of episcopal service of the poor can also be called the monastic phase. The poor figured in the Benedictine liturgy of the Washing of the Feet *(mandatum)*, when they were given alms as well; they also received charity at the gates of monasteries.

These customs were to persist for centuries. Monastic hospitality underwent enormous development, as we can see from the unusually well-preserved plan of the Abbey of Saint-Gall in Switzerland and from the regulations of some of the great monasteries. The almshouse of the poor was to be kept separate from the guesthouse, with its own special endowment, and administered by a monk whose particular task it was—eventually he had a special title. Does this mean that poverty was on the increase, or that there was greater enthusiasm for charity? There could be several explanations: population increase, technological improvements in agriculture that led in some areas to an improvement in the food of the peasants (except in years of bad harvest). Charitable effort was certainly stimulated by the teaching that charity covered a multitude of sins, but it also was weakened by inactivity, neglect and loss of interest. The feudalization of Church benefices, the unworthiness of some bishops, the decline of parish registers and hidebound attitudes in monastic almshouses, were disgraceful. Up to then, neither the isolated actions of Merovingian hermits nor the extensive voluntary poverty practiced by individuals living in the collective wealth of the abbeys could really be classed as movements of poverty. They affirmed the spiritual value of a life of poverty, as an ascesis or a test of longsuffering, and the duty of almsgiving and its salvific utility for the rich; but performing this gesture no longer seemed enough to those whose minds had suddenly and mysteriously awakened to further spiritual demands.

In effect, the true origin of the movements towards poverty from the eleventh century onwards, was the desire to conform a newly-revived spirituality to the Christ of the gospels. They certainly cannot be solely or essentially explained by economic factors. Without forgetting the yearning for ascetic purification of a man like Peter Damian, nor the demands of the Pataria in Milan, the struggle waged by the Gregorians to rid the spiritual life of its bondage to the goods of this world meant calling to witness the very sources of the spiritual life, and re-forging links with the communal poverty of the primitive Church of Jerusalem. After all, Jerusalem was what the generation of the first crusade dreamt of, the cradle of the Church, and expected to be the scene of the Last Judgment. To imitate the example of Christ and the apostles meant going out to the poor, while at the same time speaking out for them in the name of charity and of justice. The movements of poverty included several elements at the same time: the need to get rid of possessions; the contradiction between seeing material poverty as an affliction while glorifying it spiritually; the paradox of purposely choosing a lifestyle of humiliation. In short, a challenge was being hurled at one manifestation of wealth and power after another—ownership of land, the force of arms, titles, influence, money, and even learning.

Western Christianity did not, of course, have a monopoly of initiatives in regard to poverty and charity. It had much to learn from the Church in the East, with whom it was to settle its family quarrel with the conquest of Constantinople in 1204. Islam too could compare its sufis and the famous al Hallaj (so dear to Massignon) with Christian hermits and anchorites, and could present pilgrims and crusaders with the spectacle of a proliferation of hospitals and hospices medically well in advance on their Christian equivalents, provided by the generosity of believers, Westerners had to pay honour even to Hindu asceticism, when a Mendicant friar, Guillaume de Runbrouck, went to Karakorum in Mongolia, twenty years before Marco Polo set out on his travels. There was also the example of the 'black monks' of Ethiopia, in the valley of Josaphat, who so impressed the then bishop of Saint Jean d'Acre, Jacques de Vitry. This was also the period of the 'Children's Crusade' (the twentieth century would have called them 'youths'): they tried the experiment of making a pilgrimage to the Holy Land carrying neither money nor weapons, but met with disaster in Sardinia, where they fell victim to the rapaciousness of Genoese privateers. It was also during this period that St. Francis, having abandoned all his possessions to the scandal of Assisi, is supposed to have engaged in the following dialogue with Christ: 'You are mad, Francis'. 'No more than you are, my Lord'. Without a touch of such madness, the current of poverty which reached its high point in the thirteenth century, would not have become such a mighty river, whirling along and overflowing its banks. The spiritual guides of Christendom had their work cut out, trying now to embank and canalize the flood, now to set up dams. Being human, they sometimes got it wrong.

But, more important than just listing facts (already quite well known, in any case) is trying to understand what they might signify. Logical reasoning led to starting up charitable works. A kind of dialectic came into force between mysticism and action. Fed from the same source, evangelical life, the branches of the stream of poverty differed only in their development. Robert d'Arbrissel and Etienne de Muret went to seek Christ in the solitude of the forest, and they found the poor. The Canons of Prémontré, who sought a life closer to the apostolic ideal by going beyond St. Augustine's first Rule, the *Ordo antiquus*, renewed their pastoral activity in the communal poverty of the *ordo novus*. St. Bernard and St. Bruno, by proposing rigorous individual poverty ended by founding the Cistercians and the Carthusians. Arnold de Brescia and Henri de Lausanne also based their demands on the demands of the evangelical life. It was said that what made Valdès aware of his vocation was hearing the legend of St. Alexis. Was it not that same call that was heard by Durandus, by Francis and by Dominic? In le Puy en Velay, an artisan with the undistinguished name of Durandus, had a vision of our Lady, and thought up the brotherhood of the Capuchonnés which by about 1182 developed into a bloody movement. Fourteen years later, in England, another layman, William Longbeard, was led by thoughts of the Old Testament, to plan a violent rebellion for the 'deliverance of the poor', whose 'procurator' he claimed to be. People still believed in the milennium. In Calabria, that old stronghold of hermits, Father Joachim, in his monastery, announced the coming of the liberating kingdom of the Spirit. As in the parable, the wheat and the tares grew together. Which was which? It is not for the historian to decide, only to seek to understand the failures and the successes.

Some tried to sow the seed, but founded nothing. Most of the wandering preachers (Wanderprediger) left behind them only memories of their example and their influence. We know about a few hermits, but their solitude was not total; they gathered disciples around them, and they emerged from their retreats to preach penance and help the poor. Troops of beggars, vagabonds and outcasts surrounded Robert d'Arbrissel, and crowds followed Peter the Hermit. Peter left nothing behind, whereas Robert d'Arbrissel finally founded Fontevraud, and Etienne de Muret Grandmont.

Movements or institutions? How long can its own inner dynamism sustain the practice of total poverty in a form so outstanding as to give credibility to the preaching of poverty and the service of the poor? The ideal *Nudus nudum Christum sequi* was certainly not open to question, and the practice of total collective poverty was never labelled heretical. On the other hand, if anyone claimed that leading the evangelical life was enough in itself to fit them to preach, and that there was no need to become involved in the institutions of the Church, that was a different matter. Consider three examples: Robert d'Arbrissel, Valdès and Francis of Assisi. Arbrissel, a priest, received a commission from the Pope to continue preaching. He disliked building churches, not from any antipathy to celebrating the liturgy, but because he rejected all the traditional structures; in founding Fontevraud, he was establishing something special and different. Valdes was a layman, but so was Francesco Bernardone. Both decided to live as poor men with a few companions, preaching penance and helping the unfortunate. Both went to see their bishops, by whom both were at first given encouragement. But Valdes was married, and was not granted permission to leave his wife. Why did Valdes fail where Francis succeeded? Valdes thought it better to obey God than men; but for Francis, since the authority of the Pope and bishops was delegated by Christ, humility demanded that they be obeyed. That was the difference. Similarly, Durand de Huesca and the Humiliati remained in the Church, while Valdes was expelled. 'The disagreement was not over the question of poverty in itself, but over the respective functions of clerics and laymen in the Church' (A. Vauchez), and the fact that the preaching ministry called for a commission from the hierarchy. The ordination of St Francis as a deacon coincided very significantly with the authorization he received to continue his endeavour to live in poverty and preach penance.

Another aspect of the problem is the form taken by such movements. Some people would describe the foundations of Fontevraud and Grandmont, and the authorization of the Humiliati, as 'salvage jobs'; the demand that their Rules be chosen from among those already in existence was only a subterfuge. It was natural that Dominic, when he turned to action, should carry on where canonical pastoral work stopped. There is nothing surprising in the deliberate imprecision of the rules Francis made: he cared for the spirit, not the letter. He wanted to offer counsel rather than establish structures, to give his movement direction but not rigidity. Yet experience has shown the dangers of imprecision.

Over the course of time, theological and canonical thinking and discussion helped to clarify and direct action in the twelfth century, before the 'poverty debate' in the thirteenth reduced the discussion to the sterility of a schoolmen's controversy. What was the value of poverty? The fact that it was Christ's way of life made it a worthy choice for anyone, and that he had been subject to it made living in poverty a trial for salvation, and helping the poor a redemptive work. How should one live in voluntary poverty? The ideas put forward by men like Gerhoch de Reichersberg (d. 1169) led into those thirteenth-century ideas of the poor way of life. And the works of mercy, whose importance was clear from their being numbered as seven, received enrichment from the thinking of men like Gratian, Alain de Lille, Pierre le Chantre, Pierre de Blois and Raoul Ardent. A keen awareness of the sufferings of the poor meant that benevolence was based both upon justice and upon charity. The notion of 'the justice of the poor' first excused, and later, early in the thirteenth century, legitimated, theft by the poor in case of necessity. Yet despite this change of attitude, prevailing views of the poor man did not improve. He was certainly looked on as the image of Christ (Pierre de Blois called him 'vicarius Christi') but remained an object; he was there to serve his benefactor, with his prayers, in exchange for what he was given.

It is clear enough why the movements of poverty attracted laypeople. A kind of self-betterment seemed to beckon them to imitate monastic spirituality and invent a monastic spirituality of their own. Franciscan poverty attracted a great many laypeople, as is clear from the success of St Clare's order for women, as well as the Third Orders and Béguinages that grew up. Service of the poor was certainly the most highly developed form of the general movement of poverty among laypeople. Some features of it were not new: almsgiving, distributing goods to the poor, setting up bequests. The increase in donations to leper-hospitals, whose need was now greater, was very typical. One novelty was the development of real services for the poor, in which laypeople took part: hospitals in the towns, almshouses in villages, wayside hostels to shelter tramps similar to those for pilgrims, the provision of meals for the poor, good works by special confraternities. Another phenomenon of this time was the founding of congregations specifically to service the poor, such as the Order of the Holy Spirit founded by Guy de Monpellier at the end of the twelfth century, and the Orders founded to ransom captives.

The hundred years between Robert d'Arbrissel and St. Francis saw a lot of reflexion and a lot of action. Both the praises and the doubts expressed by Jacques de Vitry in his *Historia Occidentalis* about the 'poor men of Christ' seem to be justified. Without claiming that the twelfth century foresaw all the problems that would arise in the future, one can say that the experiments of the time, even the unhappy failures of the Capuchonnés or the heresiarchs, were valuable. In its return to the textual sources of evangelical poverty, twelfth-century humanism really re-read the New Testament, made a fresh direct contact with the Fathers, and returned to such neglected works as the Epistle of St. James. It became evident that in the light of these fundamental texts on poverty, fruitful protests could be made and listened to, and could inspire radical changes in behaviour. It also became clear that no movement of poverty in the Church could succeed without episcopal authorization and humility. All the movements—even before the mendicant orders came on the scene, and *a fortiori* under their influence—discovered that the service of the poor demanded that one should live among the poor as one of them. The hermits at the end of the eleventh century attempted it. Pierre de Blois recommended it: *locum elegisti ubi posses inter multos pauperes unus esse* (P.L. 207, 744). Francis of Assisi did it. The role of the laity continued to grow, but not in the modern sense of 'laicizing' the institutions of social service. It is impossible to overestimate the importance of the development towards personalizing their religious life that was experienced by the generations living during the Fourth Lateran Council; the spirituality of poverty and of charity in its social dimension became clear to them. It was both a beginning and an example.

Of course the teachings of the thirteenth century were no better followed than the examples any generation leaves for the next. The same endeavours were repeated and the same mistakes—or similar ones. It is hard to say just why this should be so. It could be changing circumstances, old solutions becoming out of date, basic principles being neglected, lack of imagination or courage, or simply the effect of routine and a certain torpor both in institutions and individuals.

Here are a few examples. Over the centuries, the marriage between the spirit of poverty and the service of the poor remains indissoluble, despite the many more or less serious ups and downs one finds in any marriage of long standing. The voluntary poverty of the mendicant orders had to face the test of time and some compromises were made—the Spirituals with systematic disputation, the Conventuals with the trappings of stability. Mendicant friars were critcized as scroungers receiving alms that should have gone to the genuine poor. Then in the fourteenth century, economic expansion followed by successive recessions, added new categories of poor people to the traditional beggars and the victims of natural disasters, of plague and of war: people who had been ruined and felt humiliated by their downfall, especially the mass of farm and craft workers. In the middle of the century, a few preachers, such as the Dominican Taddeo Dini in Florence, were denouncing injustice; but no one recognized the structural causes of poverty. Despite denunciations of avarice and of usury, the gulf between rich and poor widened. Worse still, beggars and the 'laborious poor' were lumped together as a feared and despised group and abused as 'cadgers'. They were libelled again when the revolts of the destitute were confused with subversion and heresy, in the days of Wyclif and of Huss. Thomas Brinton, a Cistercian and therefore one who had chosen poverty, as Bishop of Rochester felt he could no longer speak up for the poor after the Peasants' Revolt of 1381, even though he had always been keenly concerned with their sufferings in the past.

Setbacks of this kind can be hard to overcome. However the fifteenth century saw a renewal in the practice of religious poverty as well as in the service of the poor. The movement for nursing the sick developed. Alongside the forceful admonitions of Bernardino of Siena and the fiery discourses of Savanarola, we find doctrines of economic morality being taught by Anthony of Florence, pawnshops being set up by such people as Bernardino of Feltre, and finally, early in the sixteenth century, in large cities like Lyons, the unification of all the various welfare institutions with both clergy and laity assisting.

In the seventeenth century, the 'French school' of spirituality came into being at the same time as the charities of Vincent de Paul. The medieval idea of poverty persisted until the industrial era, which coincided in France with the restoration of religious orders after the Revolution, the social work of Ozanam, and Bishops' pastoral letters urging the faithful to respect the human dignity of workers.

What do we conclude from this brief survey? Though we only looked closely at one period, the link that can be perceived thoughout the history of the Church between the service of the poor and the spirit of poverty is the need to make oneself available to those one loves and wants to help, and to live as they do.

Translated by Rosemary Middleton

Bibliography

Etudes sur l'Histoire de la Pauvreté (Moyen Age—XVIe siècle), seminar papers from a seminar directed by M. Mollat, 2 vols. with bibliography (Paris, Publications Sorbonne, 1974); and a synthesis, *Les pauvres dans la société médiévale* (in preparation, Hachette, Paris).

M. J. Congar, *Pour une Eglise servante et pauvre* (Paris, 1963).

Povertà e richezza nella spiritualità dei secoli XI e XII (Todi, 1969).

A. Vauchez, 'La pauvreté volontaire au Moyen Age' (comments on T. Manteuffel: *Naissance d' une hérésie. Les adeptes de la pauvreté volontaire au Moyen Age*), *Annales E.S.C.* (1970) (6), 1566-73.

J. P. Guitton, *La société et les pauvres en Europe (XVIe-XVIIIes.)* (Paris, 1974).

Marie-Dominique Chenu

Vatican II and the Church of the Poor

'THE Church of the poor', 'the Church that is poor': this description is both a single and a double one—single in that the two ideas are insep-arable, yet double in the very different demands implied—and sums up perfectly one feature of the face the Church sought to adopt at the Vatican Council in an effort to be true to itself and have a livelier awareness of its true nature. 'The Church, at the Council, is looking at itself in the Gospel', was how Yves Congar put it at the time: this might seem a fairly common-place activity to some people, but in reality it was an act of renewal, since it went beyond good intentions to a real structural reform. It was therefore not just a matter of pastoral exhorta-tions to a more or less romantic evangelism: it was the very essence of the Church that was in question.

The events of the Council, and especially of the first session, made this abundantly clear. We know what a storm there was in the Assem-bly and how sharply they reacted against the schema presented to them. The pre-conciliar doctrinal Commission had in fact formulated a schema wholly constructed upon the ecclesiology taught more or less everywhere for the past three hundred years, especially in the Roman colleges: the Church is a perfect society whose work is to pass on the word of God; for this purpose she has been provided with powers of teaching and government to guarantee the truth and effectiveness of that Word; these operate through a hierarchical structure dependent on the supreme sovereignty of the Pope, which ensures the unity of the faithful and the catholicity of their faith. All this being so, Christ's coming and his grace are identified with the institution, which branches out into temporal institutions directly or indirectly influencing the workings of the City of this world—so much so that these latter institutions become the necessary and preferred channel of pastoral action. The Church, the mystery of Christ in history, is transformed into a 'Christian society', a 'Christendom', whose rights and privileges are such as to integrate its members socially and culturally into secular society, and which therefore looks upon that society as a guarantee of its own strength and stability. This solidarity of spiritual and temporal powers makes the Church appear as the guardian of the established order, which it consecrates by its presence. This concordat can, and indeed has in the past, produced disputes on the shifting boundary between the two powers; the general effect, however, is a dialogue of peaceful political coexistence, if not of a full social and cultural joining of forces.

In such a psychological and juridical situation, it is obvious that the existence, the problems, the hopes and sufferings of the poor, and even the evangelical paradox of the blessedness of poverty, will not be in the forefront. Ecclesiologists of this school will of course remember the Gospel and its hard sayings against riches and power, and will be faithful to them; but such a sanctified view of things relates only to individuals on their route to perfection, not to the Church as a visible institution, to which there is no reason to apply such evangelical concepts as humility, service or poverty. The projected schema only recalled them implicitly, in an analogy between the Church and the Incarnate Word. The questionnaire that had been sent to all the bishops before the Council certainly laid no emphasis on the 'Church of the poor'; naturally it mentioned such major world problems as hunger, poverty, labour, war, the evangelization of the poor, but none of these were seen as bound up with the structure of the Church itself.

This disjunction explains the assessment generally made of the Church's behaviour. On the one hand, it is undeniable that, throughout her history, the Church has always been a resort for the weak, the deprived, the voiceless, the poor; it has undertaken the social services that governments could not or would not perform—educating children, setting up universities, caring for the sick, sheltering the aged, and more recently, helping the handicapped—functions which, even in the industrial civilization of today, it still carries out in certain underdeveloped areas. But on the other hand, there is much truth in the received opinion that the poor receive little respect or support in the Church; there, as in society at large, they are a marginal group, and though they are certainly the objects of much praiseworthy charity, they are not acknowledged as sharing 'rights' in the name of social justice. The world of labour has come into being outside the Church, and the Church still does not know how to push her way into this vast continent of humanity. In the Church, as in political society, the poor are always a source of worry, and the powers that be keep an apprehensive and watchful eye on their complaints. 'The poor are not at home in the Church. We might as well shut up shop', was the outspoken comment of one bishop at the Council.

When the council Fathers, therefore, took to pieces the text of the preconciliar document, in their first session, to replace the concept of an authoritarian Church with that of the Church as the people of God in a community developing from the mystery of Christ, their doing so naturally awoke in them a new sensitivity to the human and evangelical problems of poverty—how to shift the emphasis from *authority* to that of *witness*, and how to fulfil the brief of preaching the Good News. In the last week of that session (2–7 December 1962), as well as the decisive interventions by Cardinals Suenens, Montini, and Frings, which shattered the whole foundation of the original document, there was a most significant statement from Cardinal Lercaro, Archbishop of Bologna: 'On reading the summary of the schemas given to us yesterday', he said, 'I was greatly surprised and upset to find something missing: among all the schemas that have been and will be presented to us, no account seems to have been taken in any document specifically and explicitly prepared in the light of the world as it is today, of one essential and pre-eminent revelation of the mystery of Christ. This was the aspect foretold by the prophets as the sign of Christ's messianic consecration, the aspect made manifest by the birth, the childhood, the hidden life and the public ministry of Jesus, the aspect that is the law and the foundation of the kingdom of God, the aspect which marks every outpouring of grace and indeed the whole life of the Church . . . We shall not be fulfilling our task properly if we do not make the centre and the soul of the doctrinal and legislative work of this Council the mystery of Christ in the poor and the evangelization of the poor. Not just as one subject among others, but as the central problem of the Council. The theme of this Council is, after all, the Church as it is, especially "the Church of the poor" '. There followed some precise practical proposals. One of the best commentators on the Council recorded the impression produced at the time: 'This intervention by the Cardinal of Bologna is the boldest and most reforming to have been made during the first session: it may well open a whole new path' (P. Rouquette, in *Etudes*, February 1963).[1]

Cardinal Lercaro was from the second session onwards to be one of the four moderators of the Council, and this intervention fell on ground that was not merely receptive but actively effective in the Assembly, thanks to a working group which had been spontaneously set up earlier on by several prelates meeting together. In fact it was at the very beginning that Mgr Hakim, Archbishop of Nazareth and Mgr Himmer, Bishop of Tournai, had distributed a short memorandum by P. Paul Gauthier (a former professor in the seminary of Dijon in France, and now a worker-priest at Nazareth) entitled *Jesus, the Church and the Poor*. On 26 October 1962, some fifty bishops and thirty *periti* met at the Belgian College; each was personally, and because of his own apostolic and national experience, peculiarly aware of the evangelical problem of poverty. In confirmation of what we have been saying, it is noteworthy that, with few exceptions, none of them were prelates from the Churches in 'Christian countries'; not, certainly, that they were lacking in individual or practical generosity, but for them 'power' had made it very hard to recognize the 'rights' of the poor.

This committee, whose existence and work remained unofficial, was nevertheless in continual contact with the Council officials. To begin with, its very effective president was Cardinal Gerler, Archbishop of Lyon; in addition it was in regular touch with Cardinal Lercaro, who himself kept the Pope informed about it. Several of its members' interventions in the Aula incorporated the committee's experiences, analyses, theories and plans into the fabric of the Council's deliberations. Several impressive documents were produced by the group, and they made a point of using the geatest tact so as not to offend the bishops of either rich countries or poor.[2]

From the first, Cardinal Ottaviani had made it known that he would include in the dossier of the commission over which he presided any suggestions that might be proposed, either in support of the role of poverty in the Church ('the Church that is poor') or for ways and means of evangelizing the poor ('the Church of the poor'). And in fact, at the second session (October-November 1963), when the new schema came up for discussion, and numerous amendments were tabled together with copious notes by various *periti*, the final statement presented a forceful theology of evangelical poverty as part of the essence of the Church (Constitution *Lumen Gentium*, n. 8, 3).

Throughout the Council, on every possible occasion, in all the various groups, references of this kind were introduced to poverty as an essential component of Christian living. Thus, in the chapter on perfection *(Lumen gentium* 42), in the decree on the Pastoral Office of Bishops (n. 13), in the decree on the Priestly Ministry and Life (n. 20), and finally, and most importantly, it is implicit in every line of the Constitution *Gaudium et spes*, especially in the section on economic life, which should be permeated with the spirit of the beatitudes (n. 72). One need only look up the word *Paupertas* in the analytical index of the official edition of the Council documents (p. 1233).

Let me quote directly from the chief text, *Lumen gentium* (n. 8), for there we find stated in forthright terms the root cause of the role played by the poor at the heart of the mystery of the Church: 'Since Christ carried out his work of redemption in poverty and persecution, the Church too is called to enter upon that path, in order to pass on to men the fruits of salvation. Christ Jesus, "though he was in the form of God, . . . emptied himself, taking the form of a servant" (Phil. 2: 6–7), and for our sake "though he was rich, yet . . . became poor" (II Cor. 8:9). So the Church, though needing human resources to fulfil its mission, was not instituted to seek the glory of this world, but to preach humility and abnegation and be an example of both. Christ was sent by his Father "to preach good news to the poor . . . to set at liberty those who are oppressed" (Luke 4:18), "to seek and to save the lost" (Luke 19:10) similarly the Church encompasses with its love all those who are bowed under the weight of human weakness; more than this, it sees in the poor and the suffering the images of its poor and suffering founder, and it hastens to ease their suffering, wishing to serve Christ in them.'

What is striking about this text, so carefully elaborated to make its meaning clear, is its essentially Christological perspective. In their concern for the sufferings of so much of mankind, and for the need to work out a better relationship between the countries where people starve and those where there is abundance, the council Fathers could have tackled these problems straightforwardly in the name of the brotherhood of man. But their demands on this head are in fact explained in terms of the working out of the 'constitution' of the Church—thereby giving them a dimension of the mystery of Christ who became poor that he might take upon himself the sufferings and hopes of the poor and the little ones. For this is, in Christ, the mystery of the Church. That mystery operates on two levels, carefully distinguished in the text: first, poverty as a way of life is an obligation laid on the Church, against all the allurements of power, as a witness to the poverty of Christ: this is 'the Church that is poor'; then, the fact that the Church's first concern must be for the poor, to whom she must preach the Good News and bring the liberation of the Messiah. He 'came not to be served but to serve' (Mt. 20:28): the Church must be a service first of all, not an authority.[3]

More and more, during the two last sessions of the Council, and especially with the production of the second Constitution on the Church in the World of Today, there came to be increasing active participation by the bishops of the poor nations, of the Third World, as it is called, working both to reinforce that mystical vision and to spell out the practical demands that follow from it. In fact a greater and more lucid solidarity gradually grew up between the bishops of rich industrialized areas and those of the developing countries. The appalling problem of the economic and political development of the world was thus reflected as a living image in the Church herself: this new awareness could only intensify the harsh words of the Gospel. We have not yet taken the full measure of the structural implications of the revolution this represented, though it was felt immediately and observed with impassioned interest.

Among the many developments during the Council, we may note the decision (which the group at the Belgian College had asked for from the first) to set up in the Church a commission to study (both centrally and in each country), the twofold problems of social and political justice. This was to become the official Justice and Peace commission. 'Justice' puts us firmly on the terrain of law—not of charity and benevolent assistance. It is evident today, and becoming more and more so, that to fulfil this brief, which forces us to shift the whole field of social morality, the Church, involved in the economic, social, political and cultural transformation of the world, is committed to the liberation of mankind.

During the fourth session, Paul VI contemplated publishing an encyclical on poverty; he discussed it with Cardinal Lercaro, who employed a number of bishops and theologians to write it. The plan came to nothing. But at Easter 1967 the encyclical *Populorum Progressio* appeared; it followed the same line of thought, outlining a programme in which arguments from the Gospel reinforced the appeal to humanity.[4] The various articles in this issue illustrate in more detail the statements and demands of that programme.

Translated by Rosemary Middleton

Notes

1. Cardinal Lercaro was to return to the same subject in a television talk on 22 December 1962 (cf. *Civiltà Cattòlica*, 114 (1963, I), pp. 285–6; and again, more fully, in a lecture given at the College of the Apostles in Juniya (Lebanon) in April 1964 (reprinted in *Eglise et Pauvreté*, Paris, 1965).

2. Any bibliography would be far too voluminous to give here. I would like, however, to mention the small work by P. Paul Gauthier, *'Consolez mon peuple'. Le Concile et l'Eglise des pauvres*, Paris, 1965, which describes the work done by the group at the Belgian College. It includes, in an appendix, a doctrinal piece by Père Congar, 'Le fondement du mystère des pauvres dans le mystère de Dieu et du Christ'.

3. To give readers some idea of the labour involved in this lengthy piece of work, I refer them to the historical study of *Lumen gentium* made by G. Alberigo and the Bologna Institute of Religious Studies, 1975.

4. In conclusion I would like to mention the text of the 'Thirteen Points by Anonymous Bishops' to the practical implementation of poverty, after returning to their respective dioceses. These commitments were made anonymously at the end of the Council, and are impressive for their clearly stated evangelical realism.

József Lukács

The Problem of Poverty and the Poor in Catholic Social Teaching

MISERY and poverty are an ineradicable human condition neither for
Marxists nor for Christians. Christianity appeared in an age when this
was already discernible on a world-historical level, but when the actual
social prerequisites for the eradication of poverty were not available.
Marxism, on the other hand, entered history in an age when the objective premises for a solution were already conceived and when con-
scientization about this situation, and at the same time the theoretical
critique and practical opposition to the social structures which ensured
the continued symbiosis of poverty producing riches and riches maintaining poverty, had become practicable.

In spite of unrelenting theoretical differences the possibilities of per-
ceptibly stronger collaboration between Christians and Communists in
many countries are favoured by, among other factors, the fact that
both are permeated by a sense of responsibility for the future of our
human world. The principle 'nil humanum a me alienum puto' was the
motto of the same Karl Marx who together with Engels wrote in the
Communist Manifesto about that future, and said that the old form of
civil society with its classes and class antagonisms was being replaced
by a form of association in which the free development of each is the
condition for the free development of all. Admittedly the authors of the
pastoral constitution on the Church in the modern world at Vatican II
were motivated quite differently when they conceived the preamble of
that important document, and remarked especially that there was nothing truly human that did not find an echo in the hearts of Christ's
disciples; they set this affirmation in a context in which this human

content was especially associated with the fate of the poor and re-pressed of all kinds.

It is clear that we are faced with a parallel set of problems leading to unavoidable dialogue.

I

It is impossible to agree with historians who declare that in the ancient East, but especially in the world of the Greek *polis*, the question of the relationship between riches and poverty and the causes of their existence, had not been raised in value terms. Yet in many books of the Old Testament we meet with an insistence not only on a religious but a social transformation which was similarly present, with, that is, the same intensity, in the Greek world only in exceptional cases. The punishment of the rich and powerful is just as strongly desired and treated as an imminent event in the human world as the liberation of the poor and oppressed.

The apocalyptic radicalism of the early Church tried to introduce this consideration into religion in the imagery of the last judgment. Engels, in his study of the early history of Christianity, said that the Book of Revelation showed that Christianity was originally also the religion of the poor and those without the law, and of the nations subjugated or routed by Rome; this opinion can hardly be refuted. Christianity, according to Engels, proclaimed an imminent liberation from the bonds of serfdom and need, and offered the feeling of being involved in a struggle with an entire world and being able to come out victorious. Accordingly there was no question as yet of a religion of love, and there was no mention of loving our enemies. John openly rejoices in revenge taken on the persecutors of the Christians.

The provisional halt to the crisis of the Roman Empire and the failure of the Jewish revolt show that radicalism was to fade. The Christian community was at a crossroads: either it was faced with certain destruction, or it had—if not to approve—certainly to acknowledge existing social conditions, certainly at first in practice and later also in theory. The Gospels and the Pauline letters show that Christianity certainly retained the Stoic notion of equality but changed it into equality in God—in guilt and redemption. Here riches are primarily an obstacle in the way of salvation, opposed to poverty which may be imbued with evil but essentially (that is, both as lack of worldly goods and as consciousness of our human weakeness) represents a more definite readiness and possibility of grace.

But it would be wrong not to acknowledge that Christianity posited the idea of equality as a goal, as equality of the faithful within a

Church. In Alfred Weber's apposite words the Church became the 'anti-form' of a social structure based on riches and poverty; it became in fact a kind of 'anti-polis' after the dissolution of the *polis*, where at least the *religious* equality of the minority of the redeemed could be realized.

In a world where no real social alternative could be discerned to the simultaneous existence of poverty and riches, the Church had only two possibilities: either it could turn its back on the 'evil' world, or it had to open up completely to the world, including the ruling classes; in that way a mission became possible and legal, and the idea of a Church active in the world yet retaining its supernatural commission could be grounded both theologically and Christologically. This meant, however, a definite break with important aspects of the ideological world of early Christianity.

After quarrels and deviations, the Church took the second way, which of course meant that soon, in economics, politics and culture, it used the means and methods of the ruling classes to increase its influence. The 'catholic' notion of university became 'Roman'. It became a community which, in addition to a feudal character, displayed several characteristics of the Roman Empire.

The judgment on poverty in the New Testament, however, was clearly contrary to the practice of the age, and always supported the protest of plebians and burghers against medieval attempts at an integrated Christian tradition. There is a continuous chain of criticism of the Church which identifies itself with the world of the rich, from the Pataria through the Cathars and Waldensians right up to Joachism; it is always strengthened by hope of a change of things as they were. The other direction of criticism was represented by the religious orders; these were for the most part mendicant orders which accepted the existing framework, but within it, through ascetic emphases in personal life, expressed their inward commitment to the Saviour who identified with the cause of the poor, and to the poor themselves.

II

According to Max Weber, Protestantism made asceticism 'this-worldly', by removing its connection with the orders. The rich Church was banished, but only to set against it the riches of the bourgeois individual which relied on thrift, the judicious application of capital, and soon the exploitation of the industrial proletariat. The Church was separated from the state and faith was partitioned off from public activity; the only consequence of this was, however, that instead of the *caritas* of medieval institutions, doing good became an *individual* moral duty, replacing bodies working to alleviate misery and suffering.

Of course the bourgeois Reformation included the protest of its ple-
beian opponents who—if we are to go by the example of Thomas
Münzer, the Anabaptist commune in Münster or the Levellers—would
not acknowledge the justice of a democratism organized by and along
church lines, the emphasis on a subjective instead of a decreed dogmatic faith, or the rôle of divine providence in salvation.

But this egalitarianism went against the profit-principle of capitalist
production. It is hardly by chance that in almost all *developed* capitalist
countries, the bourgeois-Protestant form of Christianity became the
dominant religious expression of the permanence and self-assurance of
the bourgeois order of civil society.

It was not by chance on the other hand that Catholicism, which after
the Council of Trent opposed not only the Reformation but the main
bourgeois aspirations, retained its power in the semi-feudal countries of
central and southern Europe. In that way it was able to preserve,
together with the hierarchical structure of the Church, its specific material means for the production of capital.

As a very apt judgment of J. Levada's puts it, bourgeois evolution
absorbed the Christian notion of equality, and was able to do so because in the constitution of the bourgeois rights of man, a formal,
abstract equality was the actual realization of the two modes of
equality before the law and the equality of the market. In the
nineteenth and twentieth centuries, social struggles have been and are
being conducted in which *class equality* itself and the interconnection of
poverty and riches are called in question. It is probably not accidental
that in the statements on social problems made by the leading (i.e. most
retrograde) church circles there was hardly any mention of the poverty
problem until at the end of the nineteenth century the socialist
working-class movement went beyond mere economic demands to
state its historic aims.

The encyclical *Rerum novarum* and subsquent social encyclicals are
fruits on the one hand of the new socio-political situation of the
Catholic Church, and on the other of the advancing crisis of bourgeois
society and spreading secularization which brought about a lack of
interest in religion and the growing atheism of the have-nots, the
'poor'. Perhaps it is not too fanciful to say that the great social changes
that took place in and as a result of the October revolution had to
happen, for the second Vatican Council to be stirred into declaring that
the problem of poverty was not only a conciliar problem but more
precisely *the* question itself, when it said that the scandal should be
removed of a few nations whose citizens are the majority of those
rejoicing in the name Christian, whereas others do not have enough to
live on and suffer from hunger, sickness and misery of all kinds. For the
first time in human history—the Council declared—the nations were

convinced that the advantages of civilization could and must be shared by all mankind.

The diagnosis is accurate, though some points are arguable.

The Church seems to be faced with a double task. On the one hand it is supposed to create the Church of the poor, *ad intra*; on the other, it must contribute, *ad extra*, to the removal of the scandal of poverty. It is obvious too that the Church can hardly encourage the removal of poverty without losing its economic privileges.

The real problem is what solution the Catholic Church is putting forward.

III

To answer this particular question adequately we need a lot of time. A powerful multinational organization like the Catholic Church has to take into consideration extremely diverse social presuppositions in the modern world, which means that its top bodies can only issue somewhat abstract directives.

Expositions of the poverty-riches antagonism are by no means missing from literature of Christian inspiration. In *Capital* Marx quotes the Venetian monk Ortes, who, he says, was one of the great economists of the eighteenth century, and who said that an abundance of goods always meant a lack of them for others. Ortes had discovered the core of the problem, and although the same question was put the other way around in some encyclicals, inasmuch as the simultaneous existence of poverty and riches, and of labour and capital, was derived from natural law, the constitution of Vatican II addresses with sympathy all those who wish to get rid of these shocking contrasts.

The problem of poverty and riches (that is, the way in which goods are distributed) indicates something else: distribution is a mere result of the mode of *production* which produces riches and poverty at the same time. A true critique of impoverishment is criticism of the conditions which produce impoverishment: criticism of the mechanisms which reproduce 'excess' as well as the needy, and freeze this state of things.

Christian social teaching stresses continually that *actio caritativa* should be converted into organized social action, into *actio socialis*, and severely condemns the greed-for-profit of liberal capitalism and the exploitation which springs from it. No small number of theological works warn against any sanctioning of material poverty; the Church approves of a social policy which supports economically disadvantaged individuals and nations.

Up to a point, the promotion of socio-political institutions (the support of those unable to work, invalids, the sick, widows, orphans and the aged, and so on), that is, the protection of social stability, also works to the advantage of modern monopoly capitalism. In most countries big firms try energetically to put the greater part of the burden on the shoulders of the workers themselves. That shows the class content of this form of social policy: the mere emphasis on the imperative demand for justice and love *(iustitia* and *caritas)* does not mean that any view has been expressed of contradictory social interpretations of those commandments.

One of the main sources of impoverishment until recently was unemployment—both in the developed capitalist and in the developing countries. And unemployment is something that cannot be compensated by a system of unemployment benefit or social security, however well it functions. This kind of poverty, which is obviously extremely destructive not only economically but socially, morally and socio-psychologically, is not only a result of the monopoly-capitalist mode of production but its existential condition. As Marx says, in periods of stagnation and medium prosperity this reserve army weighs on the active work force and controls its demands during periods of over-production. Attempts to remove the weight of unemployment collide at a certain point with the interests of the social order itself. The question of how ownership might favour the eradication of poverty is still open.

On the international scene, the eastern European countries, including my own country, are usually counted among the developed nations or, more precisely, the medium developed nations. However, such statistical comparisons often ignore that these countries (including Czechoslovakia and the German Democratic Republic) were among the poor countries before their transition to socialism (not without reason was Hungary known as a nation of three million beggars, and tuberculosis called 'morbus hungaricus'), and that their rise to the status of developed nation, the struggle against poverty, the complete absence of unemployment, the provision of social security, and the far from perfect yet guaranteed rise in the standard of living, are inseparable from the socialist solution to the problem of property. Therefore these countries are models of development which are worth consideration by all interested in the fight against poverty, precisely because of the extremely negative initial conditions.

Gaudium et spes acknowledges the fact that the fundamental law of human perfection, and therefore of world transformation, is the new commandment of love. But the principle of justice determines the way in which conditions are formed and perceived, including the conditions of the ownership of property. 'Therefore men must not only treat the external things that they possess duly as their personal property, but must see them as common property in the sense that those things can be of use not to them alone but to others too. In addition, all men have the right to a share of the goods of the earth which is adequate for them and their families. That was the opinion of the fathers and teachers of the Church who say that it is our duty to support the poor and not only from our surplus. Anyone, however, who finds himself in extreme need has the right to acquire what is necessary for himself from the riches of others' *(Gaudium et spes)*.

What counts as excess depends on the age, the social level and individual claims and needs. Apparently the constitutions think it is justifiable to take as is necessary from others' property only in a state of necessity. But surely mankind is in such a condition when two out of three people are needy, hungry or starving.

Conciliar constitutions and subsquent papal pronouncements do not *in principle* exclude the expropriation of goods in certain cases. Nevertheless, they still see private property as the most essential material prerequisite for the self-realization of the individual, and as the main spur to tasks and duties, and therefore as a characteristic of civic freedom.

Private property should be held in accordance with the common good. The encyclical *Populorum progressio* of Paul VI emphasizes that the right to private property is not unconditional and unrestricted for anyone, and that in certain circumstances the expropriation of the means of production could be a necessary course.

This was not the first time that an emphasis was put on the social aspect of private property in Catholic social teaching. But a statement of the possibilities of expropriation is certainly something new: an acknowledgment of the signs of the times. But the question is difficult to pursue beyond the stage of theory; what are the limits within which private property still helps the individual to be more fully himself?

Of course, for Marxists the possession of consumer goods to satisfy individual needs is the *conditio sine qua non* of self-realization. Personal property is however not the same as *private* property; its nature is to contradict the monopolist character of private property which excludes the property of others; it is not identical with the private ownership of the *means of production*. In this regard we have to ask if property is justified when it is obtained by the work of others, and not by one's own labour; when, that is, it is a means of exploitation. Does it guarantee the development of the personality in circumstances in which big, impersonal monopolies control the major sector of the capitalist economy; where, under pressure of circumstances, the individual forfeits not only his economic basis but the possibility of personal development?

The encyclical *Populorum progressio* warns in such cases against any action which might harm basic human rights and freedoms, and would seem in so doing to attribute to socialist collectivism and the planned economy a social effect that is much more attributable to the system of private property; to the system, that is, that restricts the individual excessively, and allows initiatives which, as the practice of several countries shows, limit rather than support freedom.

However complicated and difficult it is to teach men in association to take responsible and meaningful charge of the expropriated means of production and social potential, and to develop them in accordance with human needs, this is the only way in which we can find a solution.

IV

But the Christian criterion of poverty is not restricted to a stringency of material goods. Even the pastoral constitution requires the Christian to conduct himself privately and socially according to the Sermon on the Mount, but especially in the spirit of the blessedness of poverty. As Lercaro said at the Council, the Church has first to recognize that it is culturally poor.

Of course there are several interpretations of the *content* of the evangelical notion of poverty, of poverty in the Spirit. For non-believers, however, the common, rational core of these interpretations is that it would be wrong to ignore the questions of the standard of living and mass consumption, and to limit poverty to the possession of material goods.

Congar sees the meaning of poverty as its stimulus to encounter with God, although he adds that in a certain sense the love of God can be fully realized only in love of our neighbour. Both Congar and Metz examine the meaning of poverty (especially the meaning of poverty in the Spirit) in terms of Jesus's example, and both see the profound meaning of poverty as descent to the condition of the lowest, and taking uncomplainingly on oneself all the consequences of guilt, poverty and slavery, suffering and death by crucifixion, and even descent into hell, without any desire for revenge. This poverty is also an inborn characteristic of human existence: 'Every true human encounter occurs in the spirit of poverty': in these encounters we surrender a thousand other possibilities—whereas we preserve and express our own possibilities—, we acknowledge our finiteness, until finally our destiny is fulfilled in death: 'Spiritual poverty is fulfilled in obedient endurance of this profound impotence in which one no longer possesses anything but sacrifice itself, and even that only in the experience of complete loss of power'.[1]

The authentic content of spiritual poverty is, in this perspective, awareness of our finiteness, restriction and death. A Marxist feels it incumbent upon him to remark that Christian theology presents certain far from supra-historical characteristics, which were also apparent in

Christ's life, as an essential and unavoidable aspect of human destiny in this world. The death of the individual is admittedly an unavoidable necessity, yet it remains the death of the *human being*, who *acts* in full consciousness of it. Even religious belief in an infinite soul is not an expression of profound human impotence in regard to death; it includes at least just as much longing and compulsion to surmont that barrier. Impotence is not an attribute of our human existence; on the contrary, it is work, sensuous and objective activity, which continually reshapes nature, the human condition, and the human countenance; and it is in work that man appears a social being—*zoön politikon*.

Spiritual poverty, the feeling of impotence and of essential limitation are for the Marxist historical circumstances in which the *results* of human behaviour rule man as alien powers, but circumstances which can be overcome with means provided by that very development.[2]

Some Catholic theologians see this essential restriction as a starting-point (determined by original sin),[3] and see the love testified to by Christ as realizable *only within the limits of these circumstances*. The real question of the age is: Is not the Christian bound by the commandment of love to depart theoretically and in practice from circumstances which render impossible the extension of the dimensions of human solidarity: that is, of love?[4]

Though we agree with Catholics that poverty is not only a question of economic circumstances but so to speak *also of human behaviour*, and as such to be treated as social relations, we do not look on this poverty-conditioned behaviour as ineluctable fate. Marxism, as the vanguard of the revolutionary advance of the proletariat, strives to elevate the *proletariat as such* with the means offered by an alienated world—for we have no others—in a long historical process; it struggles not against the finiteness of the human individual, but against the consciousness of his *essential* restriction, *alienation* itself. Put another way, this kind of 'poverty' is not only eliminated by socialism, but realized at a higher level, inasmuch as it is countered not by the ideal of the infinity of material goods, but—on the basis of the satisfaction of material and cultural needs—the *riches of the human individual*.

'Such is the old view', writes Marx in the *Grundrisse*, 'by which man in a restricted national, religious and political mould, also appears constantly as the aim of production. This notion appears to have the advantage over the modern world where production seems to be the aim of man and riches the aim of production. But in fact, once we forget its limited bourgeois form, what is riches but that universality of needs, capabilities, satisfactions, productive forces and so on, of individuals, produced in the process of universal exchange? The full development of human control of the natural forces, both of Nature and of his own nature? The absolute realization of his creative abilities, without any presupposition other than previous historical developments, which make this totality of development, of, that is, the development of all human powers as such, measured by no *given* yardstick, an end in itself? Where he does not reproduce himself in one aspect but in his totality? Where he does not seek to remain anything that has come to be, but is in the absolute movement of becoming . . . ?[5]

Christianity was a protest against the restricted self-satisfaction of the ancient world, and can also protest against the stultification of the bourgeois world. It does *not* see the true goal of man as the possession of goods, as riches. But if Christians want to avoid extending poverty—even unwittingly— by extolling it and thus allowing it an alibi, then they must—*ceterum censeo*—investigate the actual social conditions which at this point in time encourage the development of the riches of the personality.

'In this way we all support world peace. . .' 'All men and all nations have to act in awareness of their responsibility', says *Populorum progressio*. Marxists are prepared, as they testify in the final declarations of the conferences of Communist Parties in Karlovy Vary (Karlsbad), Moscow and (East) Berlin, to advance together with those of different views along the road of discussion and resolution of problems which the forces which desire the progress of the nations could not solve (or could solve only with difficulty) without one another's aid.

Marxists and Christians who advance along that road cannot demand that one or the other should surrender their understanding of the world. But they are entitled to expect of one another that their conduct should be orientated to the interests of those millions of human beings who are denied a proper standard of living and free human development. That is also true of dialogue on poverty.

Translated by J. Maxwell

Notes

1. J.-B. Metz, *Armut im Geiste* (Munich, 1962).

2. Cf. Marx, *Economic and Philosophical Manuscripts of 1844*.

3. I am well aware that this viewpoint is much discussed at present, as was shown in discussion of the Council.

4. Dom Helder Camara's statement in this regard (quoted by Oriana Fallaci) is noteworthy: 'We clergy are responsible for the fatalism always shown by the

poor in the resignation with which they acknowledged their poverty and the backwardness of the underdeveloped nations. Here Marxists show their perception in seeing religion as an alienated and alienating force, as—in other words—the opium of the people'.

5. Marx, 'Grundrisse der Kritik der politischen Ökonomie' (draft) in: Karl Marx and Friedrich Engels, *Werke,* vol. 46, pp. 378–88.

Werner Post

A Christian Critique of Marxist
Solutions for the Problem of Poverty

I

FIRST I must correct a possible misunderstanding. Obviously Marxism is fundamentally concerned with the problem of poverty and its removal, yet it would be wrong to see it primarily as a programme that serves *only* the cancellation of material need. Even in the mid-nineteenth century this misapprehension occurred in the debate on so-called 'belly-Communism'. Some writers used this as a collective term for all political, philosophical and other critical components of socialist theories of the time so as to suggest that they arose from mere economic necessity. If that were true, when eventually it proved possible to alleviate the worst material need above all of the proletariat, the political threat of the working-class movement and the historical claim of Marxist theory to be a critique of civil society as a whole would soon be proven empty. In this perspective, Marx's entire theory is reduced to a special aspect of the 'social problem'.

Today the western industrial nations often seem to proclaim strategies for the removal of poverty which arise less from humanistic motives than from a desire to get rid of the 'spectre of Communism' in the field of international politics. Then there is a certain variety of 'philo-Marxism' which socialists also find attractive as a way of solving the problem of poverty, especially in the underdeveloped countries. Here pauperism appears as a purely regional distribution problem that could be solved in a quasi-technical manner by the application of socialist policies. It is however still implied that the removal of poverty is a separable task that can be treated so to speak away from the total context of social or even, nowadays, world order.

Any treatment of Marxist attempts to answer the problem of poverty cannot be restricted to a few technical and external aspects but must be directed to the basic presuppositions.

II

For Marxist theory, poverty is distinguished from ethical or certain religious notions in that it is not a moral problem. Marxists do not criticise or cure poverty because it contradicts a moral idea or a principle of justice. Moral considerations do perhaps have some weight in the sense of subjective motivation, but do not play an essential part in systematics or political practice, even though the meaning of implicit notions of value in Marx's theory has not yet been adequately elucidated. To that extent, those interpreters are initially justified who, as in the group centred on Althusser, maintain emphatically that Marxism has nothing in common with philanthropic humanism. Finally, there is no sure way of knowing that a world in such a condition that two-thirds of mankind live in hunger and misery is *morally* wrong. A judgment of that kind demands as a prerequisite trustworthy knowledge that the world must of its nature (as it were) be better than it is. That simply faces reality with an ideal situation: what ought to be. Essentially it offers no more than a call to action, an affirmation of good will, or the eliciting of guilt feelings.

It is better to reconcile ideas of what ought to be with real possibilities; this should be more than a mere intellectual accommodation. One would have to show whether there is an historical dynamics resulting from the impoverishment of the greater part of mankind, and producing (by its own power, as it were) forces which enable that misery to be surmounted. If an attempt to discover that dynamic process in reality proves successful, then no appeal to morality is necessary. The argument would not be ethical but historico-material, and refer not to a condition of amorality but to one of historical contradictions.

III

The practical inconsequentiality of moral criticism is easily shown in various ways. In view of the hardly diminishing and in fact increasing poverty in the world, however, any confidence in a real dialectics of riches and poverty seems quite ludicrous.

But it is not a question either of conceptual and idealistic solutions or of historico-mechanistic constructions. In the *German Ideology* Marx referred to historical science as the unique science, because it starts from the actual process of real life, and does so in two senses: it begins with material reality, the conditions of the production of life; and it conceives reality as a process: that is, every historical circumstance is a result; nothing is of its nature as it is, for it has always come to be what it is. Hence the circumstance of the distribution of poverty and riches is also a historical result, the consequence of human action, and therefore something which is essentially changeable. That is an inescapable presupposition of historico-materialist dialectics. The distribution of poor and rich depends less on natural factors than on the actual form of society. So long as production occurs under strict conditions of scarcity, domination is inavoidable. But in the era of capitalist production stringency seems to be at an end; riches for all seem possible and domination seems superfluous.

Of course Marx did not stop at these general presuppositions, but tried to delineate the capitalist dynamics of self-surpassing progress. As is often said, this dynamics ultimately depends on the contradiction of capital and labour. Its goal is the transition from private control of the means of production to social control. That would remove the antagonism of property-owning and impoverished classes, and solve the problem of poverty. Hence poverty is not a natural category but something that can be determined only within the context of whatever riches are historically possible in particular circumstances (apart, of course, from the absolute minimum essential for sheer existence).

In his work on the theory of labour value Marx develops the idea that is constitutive for his theory: the notion, that is, that the proletarian, merely in order to live, has to sell his only means of production, his own labour power. For that he receives the usual market price, his wages. So far, he is not 'cheated'. The capitalist, however, in the same working period earns from his work force more than it costs him in wages. In that way he produces excess value for his own profit and becomes increasingly rich without the worker obtaining any surplus value for himself; relatively speaking, in fact, the worker gets poorer. Therefore riches depends on the exploitation of the work force.

In order to increase profit, the capitalist has to rationalize production. Above all he has to reduce wage costs by rationalization. At first that causes unemployment and low wages, but also leads (because automated production is only profitable with the manufacture of large numbers of items), under competitive conditions, to overproduction. Since mass consumption fails as a result of unemployment and so on, overproduction and underconsumption occur simultaneously, and a crisis results. Attempts are made to overcome it by cutting overcapacities and concentrating on non-competitive oligopolies or monopolies and the opening up of new markets. Hence the necessity for capital ultimately to expand globally, and even to abandon national frontiers. Its does not remain confined to an economic form of expression but assumes a political or military form. In spite of this worldwide spread the inherent contradictions remain unresolved. Therefore we can quite consistently see the present conflict between the rich industrial states and the underdeveloped poor countries as the globalization of a class antagonism that was formerly restricted to one society. Class warfare begins when the countries of the third world begin to organize themselves politically and no longer continue, for instance, to sell their raw materials at low prices just as the nineteenth-century proletarian sold his labour power. The shock of the so-called 'oil-crisis' in Europe shows how subject to crises the present system of the distribution of poverty and riches is.

IV

Admittedly the techniques used to combat crises have been considerably refined in the last few decades. They concern especially the complicated field of state and production. In spite of flexible crisis-management, there is still considerable doubt whether they are anything more than delaying tactics; however, I cannot go into this question in any more detail here. It is undeniable, nevertheless, that the well-being of a minority is bought at the expense of the need and suffering of the greater part of mankind.

Another, more important aspect of poverty is that instead of having continually to discover new markets, the turnover of goods can be increased just as much by the creation of artificial demands. Then increased consumption produces an appearance of well-being; in fact material poverty no longer plays a decisive rôle in our part of the world. But under the heading of 'alienation' the young Marx had already developed a non-material concept of poverty. Under the conditions of capitalist production, so Marx shows, life must ultimately become a means of living. Labour no longer has anything to do with the self-development of the individual and species forces. Internal and external nature submit to the exploitative character of all production. The isolation of private production is lastingly internalized. Disturbances in communication show what happens when human relations take on the character of exchange value and people treat one another as if they really were mere commodities.

Just as the capitalist as an individual cannot escape this deformation, so rich countries cannot evade this form of impoverishment. Still worse, even where people no longer share the illusion that consumption compensates them for such poverty, various anti-repressive measures show the social totality of alienation. This extends from the 'humanization of the world of work' right up to sexual liberation; in the form of 'repressive desublimation' (Herbert Marcuse) these ventures also usually bear the stigma of a subtle form of impoverishment. Something similar occurs when, in spite of external liberality, real impotence in regard to any influence on political decisions is experienced as poverty. This also occurs in most socialist societies.

Poverty in the Marxist sense is therefore a qualitative problem. Even a high standard of living does not mean that poverty has been conquered. Yet the reverse is not true. To overcome poverty a relative degree of riches is always necessary.

V

Christian criticism of Marxist attempts to solve the problem of poverty is often too glibly directed against the practice of socialist countries. Anyone who experiences, say, Vatican pomp, or who remembers the long complicity of the Church with the rich classes; whoever sees well-fed prelates allowing themselves to be persuaded to lecture on the virtue of poverty; whoever is aware of the Church's record as an employer, can think of bodies more fit to judge the problem of poverty. The Marxist criticism of religion has expressed itself very clearly on Christian suggestions of this kind.

At the same time it is impossible to overlook a certain affinity of Christianity and poverty. The birth of Jesus in a manger remained a major *topos* in spite of all the attempts at divinization, and it is beyond question that he was closer to those who are burdened and heavy-laden, closer to the manger than to the palace. Jesus never cites riches as a sign of divine election.

It has never been possible really to maintain that poverty is a punishment sent from God; the idea of acceptable poverty depends of course on the conviction (with a metaphysical as well as eschatological basis) that this world remains transitory and imperfect. This poverty underwent a symbolic elevation; it expressed in a perceptible form the need of an entire world for redemption. The fact that need and suffering exist loses in scandal value if that is the case, for even riches appear as a transient deception, and property is only a divine good which human beings are allowed to administer. The alleviation of the worst consequences of poverty is a task of love for our neighbour.

If we forget for a moment the freely chosen, spiritually conscious poverty of the great Orders, then two main lines can be distinguished in the Christian understanding of poverty. One comes from the love ethic of the Sermon on the Mount which offers an absolute cancellation of the opposition of poverty and riches; then there is the theory of the transient nature of the world in which poverty has always to be taken into account, since the completion is still to come on account of which (however) these problems seem less serious. Theologically speaking, both lines could be reconciled in, say, a special Christology; that would not remove the need to find an appropriate practical form. In history Christianity has often refused or failed in precisely this task. Actual forms of Christian social behaviour are as far behind doctrine as doctrine is still inappropriate to credible practice.

VI

Neither Christianity nor Marxism conceives poverty as a strictly moral problem of social injustice. Theology works from the basis of an incomplete or imperfect reality which cannot be lastingly alleviated even through fraternal solidarity and technical progress. Even in Marxist doctrine there are similar sceptical traces which do not, however, refer to poverty. As the result of actual historical processes poverty seems eradicable; but a transient metaphysical accident which has set the world awry, is sheer speculation as far as Marxism is concerned, and can only lead to a relaxation of practical efforts.

Of course Christians do not see the world only as a fatal process, but try to ensure that a new quality apparent since and with Jesus in history itself (as its inner possibility)—love—prevails against the fatalism of the old eon. To that extent the eradication of poverty is basically a Christian aim, though of course it is not restricted to any fixed forms; the age of almsgiving is certainly past, even though little more than a few experiments and a general motivation to get rid of poverty are to be discerned as yet. But there is also the assurance that all is not lost even if this task remains unaccomplished in the end.

For Marxism the mere attempt to do one's best against poverty counts for little in the long run. The result is all; either poverty is banished and the compulsion to pauperization is cancelled, or not. The consistency of the materialist viewpoint is apparent here. If poverty seems so to speak ineradicable as a *conditio humana,* then Marxist theory itself would be fundamentally questionable. To judge it at this stage is speculative procedure, however, for truth is revealed in practice.

VII

Since there is still poverty in, as it were, abundance, it is permissible for Christians to ask whether history does not argue against the Marxist interpretation of impoverishment. But of course historical reality can just as easily be used to argue against Christianity itself. We have to ask whether Marxist concepts are adequate in the present; in, that is, a time that occurs before the complete removal of poverty in a revolutionary era.

For a long time Marxists have entertained discussion of the 'subjective factor'; in short, how individual aspects of a Communist can come into conflict with the objective logic of development. Even the fact that this discussion has proved necessary is significant. If we apply this point to the question of poverty, we must ask to what extent human misery, if it is primarily an expression of universal social contradictions, has to be refined within the context of a theory of catastrophe, in order to provoke the contradictions appropriately? Even Marx and Engels approach this kind of strategic instrumentalization when they talk about the function of the 'lumpen-proletariat' (in themselves of no revolutionary value). The Christian requirement to attend even to the least of one's brethren is more relevant in this regard, though in no way safe from functionalization.

Marx begins *Kapital* with a very significant statement on the 'riches' of societies which follow the capitalist mode of production. In principle a historical stage has been reached in capitalism in which the welfare of all is possible and the 'prehistorical' age of scarcity is at an end. Poverty is merely a distribution problem, and ultimately, therefore, one of domination—which of course establishes the entire production process. There are many indications that here Marx was subject to an optimistic illusion about the nature of progress. The expansion of capital and the industrial techniques which it has liberated have affected the natural basis of the production of well-being more severely than was once conceivable. It is possible that the eradication of the capitalist mode of production will have to take place not in terms of the equable distribution of riches, but of poverty, if the living standards of the most developed countries are used as a criterion. At least a renewed attempt is needed to decide what poverty and riches could mean under these actual presuppositions. Then certain Christian pronouncements on the impossibility of changing a basically inadequate situation will be more relevant and, once deprived of dogmatic clothing, their sober lack of illusion will correct far too lofty Marxist expectations of the complete eradication of poverty.

Translated by V. Green

Ronaldo Munoz

The Function of the Poor in the Church

THE first thing to establish, as I see it, in writing on a theme such as this in an international journal with aspirations to universality, is where one is writing *from*. In a world such as ours, economically held together by inequality and unjust structures, as we know, one's personal situation cannot fail to affect one's view of the overall problem.

Rational discussion—*logos*—undoubtedly both can and must aspire to universal validity. But when—as with all Christian *theo-logia*—we are dealing with the *logos* about a God-with-us, our speculation will be vain and futile unless it expresses a living experience. And experience of the *God of the poor* will differ according to whether one lives it as someone called to it from a world outside, or as an all-embracing reality from within the world of the poor; just as one's experience of the *Lord of the Church* will differ according to whether one's daily reference point is a Northern European parish, or a popular base community in Latin America.

Well, I am writing from a working-class 'township' or suburb of Santiago de Chile. This means that my viewpoint is not that of an industrialized North Atlantic country—the 'First World' of the rich nations, even with their poor sectors, minorities alienated to a greater or lesser degree; it is that of a country of the under-developed continent of Latin America—part of that 'Third World' of the *poor nations,* though with its wealthy minorities, who have to be characterized as not-the-people.

So now we are in this Third World of the poor nations, we must at once ask what *sort of Church* we are talking about. The question of what function the poor can or should perform in the Church cannot be divorced from the other question of what sort or part of the Church they are to perform it in. And the answers to both will vary according to the particular type of Church the poor find themselves in.

If it is a *colonial* type of Church, the poor will exist in it merely as the clientele or faithful of a socio-economically alien clergy. In this case, they will be passive beneficiaries of the religious services and charitable and educational programmes of a Church personnel who remain alien to the people. In this case, it is virtually impossible to think of any active function they can perform, or influence they can have, on the non-poor of the Church, that is, on the clergy and their auxiliaries, and on the colonizing classes or nations from which these come[1].

But if it is an *autochthonous* Church—or one to the extent that it has become, at least—then the poor will have become the active subject of the Church in that place, despite the presence of brethren from overseas, who will in any case have tried to assimilate themselves to the socio-cultural *mores* of the people. In this case, the poor will not merely be recipients of the Church or in the Church: they will *be* the Church—a Church re-created in the situation of this poor people and with the values of their culture.[2] Then the poor, formed into a base or local Church, can and in fact do fulfil a function of vital importance in relation to the non-poor of that local Church and the non-poor Churches of the world: that of *prophetic denunciation* of materialist possessiveness, of the injustices and divisions that today tear humanity apart. More important still, perhaps, they have a function of *evangelical annunciation*—proclaiming a renewed experience of Christian brotherhood, and active commitment in a history of liberation inspired by hope in the Kingdom of God. But, if we are to gain a better idea of what this means, we have to look closer at how the poor of the Church of these parts have come to find themselves in the situation of being able to play this rôle.

THE SITUATION OF THE CHURCH OF THE THIRD WORLD

In the Church of the Third World, the renewing dynamism of the Council has shown itself in a significant advance on the road away from colonial Church towards autochthonous Church. In Latin America, this advance has been brought about by an opening—in many cases an 'exodus'—of the Church away from the wealthy classes toward the world of the poor majorities. Significant people and groups belonging to the wealthy classes—priests and religious in particular—are drawing close to the poor in a new way, many of them becoming part of the urban or rural proletariat in order to share the situation, hopes and struggles of the world of the people, and to proclaim in it the liberating message of the Gospel. And in response to this movement, the workers themselves, shanty-town dwellers and rural poor alike, are forming themselves into groups and community centres, which on one hand are developing an increasing network of organization at popular level and on the other becoming more organically linked to the parishes and the rest of the traditional framework of the Church. These communities are re-discovering the warmth of Christian brotherhood, reading the good news Jesus preached to the poor in a fresh way, and in a meaningful situation, and developing a consciousness of belonging to a people with a history of oppression and a vocation to freedom—taking on the mission of being the leaven of the Kingdom of God in the mass of the people.

In this way we have reached a situation where *two models* of the Church exist side by side, with a greater or lesser degree of communication between them. These models are distinguished precisely by their relationship to the world of the poor and the place that the poor can find in each type. Not two Churches, of course, but two levels or sectors of the same Church, each with its distinctive ecclesial experience and pastoral practice, which imply two distinct ecclesiological outlooks.

On one side, there is the model of the 'great institutional' Church, with its sociological and cultural centre outside the world of the poor, in the rich sectors of the country and the rich nations of the world; a Church that values discipline more and seeks greater functional cohesion; that practices organized aid to the poor; a Church with the power to negotiate with political and military authorities and exercise some pressure on them in order to obtain an amelioration of the social conditions brought about by the régime; a Church that teaches doctrine with authority and can make itself heard through the mass media of communication.

The other model is that of the 'communications-network' Church, with its sociological and cultural centre in the world of the poor, among the poor who make up the bulk of the population of this country and of the poor countries of the world; a Church that values fraternity more and looks for a greater sharing of responsibility; that lives and preaches solidarity in the midst of the people, fulfilling its rôle of prophetic denunciation of injustice, discreetly maybe, but still accepting the concomitant risks, so as to awaken a consciousness of their dignity in the poor together with hope for a better world; a Church that, in and from the world of the poor, seeks to bear witness to the Gospel, generally without disposing of any means of communication beyond person-to-person contact.

So we have two different schemes for the relationship between the Church and the world. Both include socio-cultural relationships of belonging, or at least of assimilation, and socio-political commitment and interaction. But the 'world', in these parts, is characterized by a violent contrast between the standard of life of the privileged few and that of the majority, by an economic system that places the natural and human resources of our countries at the service of the profit and well-being of the minority, by a series of cultural overlays and a political system that alienate the majority from the possibility of expression of and participation in the decision-making process. So we should not be surprised that the incarnation of a Church in a 'world' of this sort is bound to result in an ecclesial reality of extremes, those extremes in conflict with each other. The two levels of Church I have distinguished will each have a different relationship with the world, or at least will each approach that relationship in a different way.

In the first case, the 'great institutional' Church will relate to the 'world', or to global society, in the guise of a nation, starting from the top: the wealthy classes and the State. The relationship between this sort of Church and the people, or popular classes, will to some extent be a copy of the paternalist, centralist pattern of relations between the 'top' and 'bottom' of society within each nation; it will be a *teaching* Church, one that prescribes, that hands over goods and services to the poor *for* the poor, but not *from* the poor or *with* the poor.

In the second case, on the other hand, the 'communications-network' Church will relate to world society from the bottom: the world of the poor. Because its stance is one of solidarity with the poor, its word will tend to mainly prophetic denunciation of injustice and proclamation of the good news of the brotherhood of the sons of God, its action will be directed above all to sharing between brothers and together building a world more in keeping with the will of the Father. The relationship between this Church and the wealthy classes and the State will start from the situation of marginalization that characterizes the position of the poor majorities in relation to the socio-economic and political peaks of our nations; its attitude to these will be formed in the context of social criticism, liberating struggle and quest for a new society—the attitude proper to the most conscientious sectors of the people. It follows that the reaction of the wealthy classes and the State to this communications-network Church will tend to be either the distant toleration or the repression which, in our countries, is typical of their reaction to any popular organization that implies a consciousness of oppression and a course of action designed to chance the situation.

INTERACTION BETWEEN THE TWO MODELS

Having established that there are two types of Churches, corresponding to two levels or sectors of one particular Church, we must not lose sight of the fact that each inter-relates and interacts with the other. It is important, too, to see this interaction in the historical framework of the dynamic post-conciliar renewal of the Church in Latin America. The establishment and development of the 'communications network' among the people could not have come about—where it has—without significantly altering the attitude of the Church that has remained in the centre of society as 'great institution'. This aspect is vital to my theme here, since it largely conditions the possibility of the active function of the poor in the Church being exercised beyond the confines of the working-classes of this continent, working as a projection into the universal Church and contributing to its purification and enrichment.

Now it must be said that the *evolution of local Churches* since the 'little Council' of the Medellín Conference, has been at least unequal, if not downright divergent.

In many cases, Medellín has brought about a pretty deep change of attitude on the part of the 'great institution' and a significant reorientation of its pastoral approach: a change and reorientation that have taken shape in real support for the growth and liberating practice of the communications networks that have sprung up among the people, while at the same time feeding on their experience and witness. To the degree that this has happened, the Church's commitment to and interaction with the ruling classes have of necessity weakened, leading to a situation of conflict, with various degrees of latency or openness. At the same time, the Church's presence among the poor has been deepened and strengthened, since the communities are better linked and better equipped for organic and steady growth, being able to show themselves to the people not as marginal groups, but as a form of the presence and commitment of the great Church, the Church becoming the mouthpiece of those who have no voice and the proclaimer of the Gospel to the poor.

In other cases, the sectors of the Church remaining at 'the centre' have made no more than a superficial, even merely verbal, commitment to the principles of Vatican II and Medellín. In these cases, the 'exodus' to the world of the poor and the growth of new ecclesial communities in it are approved only 'on principle'. Their true quest is not followed, their re-reading of the Gospel not understood, nor the social commitment that follows from it taken on. When this happens, the new communities remain on the fringe of the great institution, and their relationship with it tends to degenerate into conflict or breaking away. Then the communities are deprived of the ecclesial roots and support they need to guide and legitimize their search for new ways, and the institution is deprived of the spirit of prophecy that should be helping it to emerge from its present commitments and open itself up to the world of the poor with a new pastoral approach and a more evangelical outlook.

THREE FACTORS NECESSARY FOR INTERACTION

Summing up, one can point, in the light of the historical experience of Latin America, to three factors necessary for the poor to fulfil an effective function of evangelical renewal, which must all come together: the values of the world of the poor, the Christian communities acting as sign and leaven in the dough, and the great institution of the Church dedicated to the service of the communities among the people.

The Values of the World of the Poor

In Latin America, it is an incontestable fact that the bulk of the population suffer from social structures and particular acts of oppression that force on them a denial of justice and a fragmentation of their solidarity. What is perhaps less obvious to those living outside is that the same people also possess—together with a religious faith—a vague but deep feeling of being loved by God, of being called to communion with him precisely because they do not take account of the riches, wisdom and power of this world, but care more for the love of the brethren and the equal dignity of the sons of God. This consciousness of brotherhood and of a call to freedom, rooted as it is in Christian evangelization, can clearly be seen to follow in the Biblical tradition of the alliance of God with his oppressed people, culminating in the suffering on the Cross. This consciousness can be seen expressed in some of the collective acts of the people—in religious festivals as well as in the class struggle and their daily solidarity with their neighbours and workmates—even in some that seem to bear little relation to Christian orthodoxy and orthopraxis. But the expression is ambiguous and the practice imperfect, since they exist in a climate of oppression and within a dominant culture that together block the historical thrust of the Christian faith toward the integral liberation of man and the building of a society based on justice and brotherhood.

The Christian Communities as Sign and Leaven

If the paschal dynamism of the Christian faith is to be historically effective among the people, this can only come about through the appearance among the people of communities living this faith with clearer consciousness and more commited responsiblity than the mass. In a situation of captivity, *diaspora* and ignorance, implying an objective alienation from the God of the Exodus and the Passover, the Christian community must appear among the people as prophetic critic and effective sign of a new brotherhood, a brotherhood rooted in the experience of the universal fatherhood of the God of Jesus Christ. But if they are to perform this function, these communities cannot be imposed and pro-grammed from outside. Even if they need pastoral agents from outside, they must arise and take their shape from the world of the poor itself; only by belonging to this world and being committed to it can they discover their prophetic mission and this new brotherhood, through a re-reading of the Gospel of Jesus from within their historical situation, through an interpretation of their oppressed situation in the light of the Gospel, through a new understanding of the values and vocation of the people.

The Great Institution at the Service of the Communities

These Christian communities can really only take root in the people through the agency and with the support of pastors sent from estab-lished centres in the countries concerned or from other countries where the Church is established with a more institutionalized consciousness of the true tradition that goes back to Jesus Christ. The communities and groups that spring up among the people need the help of the 'great institution' if they are to stay linked to the great Christian tradition (catholicity in time) and to the universal presence of the Churches throughout the world (catholicity in space). And—more specific to the theme of this article—the experience and prophetic-sacramental mis-sion of the communities need the aid of the 'great institution' if they are to overcome the dispersion and marginalization characteristic of the world of the poor, let alone to evangelize the wealthy sectors of society and force a change in the socio-economic and political structures cur-rently in force in this country, throughout this continent and in the world as a whole. But the 'great institution', in its turn, can only lend this support, perform this mission of linking the popular communities together and projecting their message, insofar as it has a clear commit-ment to their mission, and allows itself to be questioned and renewed by their evangelical experience, rooted as it is in the values and histori-cal situation of the poor of the earth.[3]

In conclusion, I should like to stress two basic aspects of the message the poor—insofar as they conform to the values I have set out—bring to the Catholic Church and its witness today. These aspects can be summed up in two words: *brotherhood* and *hope*.[4]

In the conditions of marginalization and loss of human dignity im-posed on them by the ruling socio-economic and cultural structures, the poor continue to share their goods, their sorrows and their joys with their neighbours and workmates; at the same time, they are finding new forms of grouping and community, in which each person can once again find his face and his voice, and Christians can rediscover the real brotherhood of the followers of Jesus sharing out their experience of the Father.

In the conditions of injustice, oppression and captivity imposed on them by the ruling systems and their police support, the poor continue to believe in the possibility of a world of justice and freedom; many of them carry on fighting for it, and Christians can here find once more a historical commitment to the God who made an Alliance with his oppressed people, who offered them a goal of justice and integral liberation at the end of their march.[5]

Translated by Paul Burns

Notes

1. The Second General Assembly of the Latin-American Episcopate, held at Medellín in Colombia in 1968, used the terms 'internal colonialism' and 'external neo-colonialism' in its analysis of the socio-economic, political, cultural and religious state of this continent, although it consists of countries with a century and a half of political independence behind them. (cf. *Medellín: Conclusiones*, chs. 2, 4, 6.)

2. The theme of the *autochthonous Church* played an important part at the last Synod of Bishops (1974), mainly thanks to the efforts of the African bishops. It found a modest place in the Final Declaration (n. 9), and was taken up more explicitly by Paul VI in his *Evangelii Nuntiandi* (nn. 62–63).

3. Ever since Jesus preached the good news of the Father's love to the poor and sinners of his day, in contrast to the established Judaic framework, the Church has been continually challenged to *escape from its own establishment and go out to the world outside*. Not only so as to take the Gospel to this world in a form already familiar to the Church, but also to rediscover the essence of its message as it is faced with it in its particular historical embodiment, with an invitation to break its familiar framework in order to build a new catholicity with the help of outsiders. This is what happened with the Gentiles in the time of Paul; with the Germanic and Slav barbarians in the time of Boniface, Cyril and Methodius; with the Indians of America in the time of Las Casas; now, with the poor of the world. (Cf. Synod of Bishops, 1971, *Justice in the World*, particularly the Introduction and final chapter.)

4. Cf. *ibid.*, final chapter.

5. The *base ecclesial community* and the *integral liberation of man* were two more specific themes dealt with at the last Synod, in the context of general evangelization of the world of today. They were themes introduced mainly by the bishops of Third World countries, and again taken up by Paul VI in *Evangelii Nuntiandi* (December 1975).

Bibliography

L. Boff, *Teología desde la Cautividad* (Bogotá, 1975).

J. Comblin, *Teología de la Misión* (Buenos Aires, 1974).

A. Cussianovich, *Desde los Pobres de la Tierra. Perspectivas de Vida Religiosa* (Lima, 1975).

P. Fontaine and R. Muñoz, *Nuestra Iglesia Latinoamericana. Tensiones y Quehacer de los Cristianos* (Bogotá, 1975).

S. Galilea, *A los Pobres se les anuncia el Evangelio?* and *A dónde va la Pastoral?* (Bogotá, 1975).

G. Gutiérrez, 'Praxis de Liberación y Fe cristiana', in *Signos de Liberación* (Lima, 1973).

J. Marins and team, *Modelos de Iglesia y Comunidad Eclesial de Base en América Latina* (Bogotá, 1976).

C. Mesters, 'O futuro do nosso passado', in *Uma Igreja que nasce do Povo. Comunidades eclesiais de base* (Petropolis, 1975).

A. Methol Ferré *et al.*, *Pueblo e Iglesia en América Latina* (Bogotá, 1973).

R. Muñoz, *Nueva Conciencia de la Iglesia en América Latina* (Salamanca, 1974).

CLAR team of theologians, *Tendencias Proféticas de la Vida Religiosa en América Latina* (Bogotá, 1975).

Hubert Lepargneur

The Problem of Poverty and How the Church Can Help

THERE is a wide distinction between the wealth or poverty of the Church at the same time in different places, as if there were no agreement about the spirit of the Gospel on this question. Historically the distinction has widened. At the extreme two different forms of organization produce two quite different mentalities. Two different concepts of the Church have arisen from two different frames of mind created by the local history of the place where the Church is established. These two mentalities sometimes clash, particularly in the missionary areas of the Third World. With this in mind this article suggests a closer look at: (1) *the inevitability of a real antagonism* between the prophetic-utopian pole of the Church and the Church as it is in a world where free gifts are suspect and institutions are judged by their fruits in history; (2) *the development of scales of value* which profoundly affect the problem of poverty today; (3) *the need for constant confrontation* between ends and means in the Church as an institution and Christian life; (4). *the tasks proper to the Christian community* in this area. The problem of poverty in the Church is a practical one and the particular context is relative to this. First let us consider the terms of the dilemma which is a particular instance of the general dialectic between a morality based on principles or intentions and the ethics of results.

THE FUNDAMENTAL DISCREPANCY

The 'Powerlessness' of Poverty

Poverty does not exist as such. Poverty is people experiencing the lack of the necessities of life, and the necessary means to acquire them, experiencing being poor. As a human phenomenon poverty can be defined as powerlessness, incapacity. It can be contrasted with other socio-economic states, but also includes a strong psychological element. As the powerful tend to relate to each other, notably by infiltration and exchange, the poor are not poor of their own free will.

This negative definition also has a positive aspect: poverty includes hope of making real progress. Poverty is the dynamism of the process of liberation. Wretched conditions of life are merely dead weight, crushing the spirit. Poverty, which apart from the fact that it may often be regarded as temporary, is compatible, even connected with freedom of spirit, warmth of heart, the health of the soul and spiritual joy. The positive aspect of poverty is always linked to the idea of freedom. In terms of liberation, humanization and Christianization have two sides: liberation from the obsession with wealth (what one has or has not) and liberation from the slavery of grinding need.

The 'Power' of All Organizations, Including the Church

Once it decides to become a visible society, the Church, the community of believers, cannot escape the problems facing every institution: organization, hierarchy, administration which tends to grow ever more complicated, increasing wealth. It would be unrealistic to deny this aspect of the Church's existence in the world. In fact nobody disputes the Church's right to have material needs and obtain satisfaction for them from its members.

Spiritual powers have temporal implications. These have decreased with the growth of secularization but they still exist. The attainment of religious ends requires the erection of buildings, the employment of personnel, the holding of meetings, the performance of rites, which all cost money. In order to do its work the Church has, as well as its spiritual powers and its members, goods and know-how (hard ware and soft ware).

Refusing to Come to Purely Verbal Agreement

'Poverty of spirit' has an important place in spirituality but is not a sufficient basis for the Church in the socio-economic order. The possession of wealth by proxy, or physical or moral 'persons', is no longer an adequate way of justifying the *status quo*. Organisations representing the Church still often hold enormous wealth both in developed and under-developed countries, particularly in Latin America. This is widely known although the details are not publicized. Public opinion is rightly less concerned about the amount of wealth accumulated by a religious organization and the economic power this gives it, than about the way in which this capital is used. Does the Church use it simply to enrich itself or to serve the common good and in particular to help the poor?

Ecclesiastical pronouncements and speeches are often evasive on this point. However the public is not unaware of it. This conspiracy of silence glosses over certain important discrepancies. How is it possible to develop true *brotherhood* while maintaining the inevitable social hierarchies and the structural conflict they involve? How is it possible to preach *equality* respected neither by capitalism nor communism? How is it possible to promote *freedom* which the Church itself has frequently abused? What the Church proclaims inseparable from what it *does*. In each case a balance must be found between prophetic declaration (a denunciation and call to re-construct) which is often merely utopian and practice which aims at being realistic but which is often merely self-interested?

DEVELOPING VALUES

The Modern Ethos Encourages Efficiency

In the present very rapid transformation of systems of value, it is difficult to tell how far the Gospel values should adapt to modern cultural changes and when they should stand firmly against them, because they express 'the spirit of this world'. Both extremes of rigidity and slavish imitations are certainly to be avoided.

I am not questioning the mystical inspiration of Christian poverty, which in any case is never simply a factual situation. The *kenosis* of the incarnate word, the imitation of Christ poor and crucified, identification with the most deprived who need the Gospel, will always inspire Christian poverty. However it is more useful today to turn our attention towards poor *people* rather than the myth of poverty. We should adapt the message to respect the absolute value of human persons in their relative situations and various callings.

The modern ethos exists and the Church cannot simply disregard it. The power of poverty as a sign has decreased in modern society, both among the rich and among the poor. If we add one more poor person to the mass of the poor we'll very probably get nothing more than this mass with one more added to it. Poverty has no prophetic force except in sermons. Even in traditionally Christian areas none of the three vows of religion is respected and valued in the same way as it was even thirty years ago. This is not a reason to abandon these vows but it does mean that their social value must be reassessed. We must decide whether they are *efficient*, particularly in the Third World.

Poverty as the Price and Condition of Witness rather than its Substance

Particularly among the poor, poverty does not usually bear witness to anything. Neither does the witness of poverty affect the rich. Rich people talking about poverty have even less impact. However this new ethos does not entirely discount the value of evangelical poverty, which is often the *price of bearing witness* because anyone who covets power, advancement, money or position does not have the inner freedom needed to bear true witness to justice and the Gospel. Or else evangelical poverty is the *necessary condition for being listened to* in certain contexts. The world expects the Church and its clergy to speak more truly, live more authentically, work more effectively to help the oppressed and the weak, rather than just be poor themselves. In Latin America the poor are often deprived of their goods to decorate churches and endow the clergy. They have never demanded that their priests should be poor but that they should be upright and devoted.

The Christian Assumption of this Ethos with Liberation in View

The theology of liberation has arrived, and about time too, to denounce the centuries during which the Church did not seem to care about anything except the extension of its own influence. This theology only remains Christian if it does not become an idolatry of visible short or long term efficiency. Faith is the touchstone of cultural values. It assimilates them and then puts them in their place in a total scale of values. The effectiveness of the Gospel does not coincide exactly with any form of worldly efficiency. The poor have first place and the Church must not deny the struggles of the past about which it was silent (class struggles, hostility between races and nations). But the Gospel preaches the total liberation of all mankind. In the matter of poverty 'witness' comes from an inner life, a true spirituality and personal choice of values. A Christian does not display his poverty, he simply lives with it. But he must be able to show his teeth in defence of the human rights of *others:* in this case efficiency is a paramount requirement.

THE FUNCTIONS OF THE CHURCH

The Church must assume poverty in a way which will help it to do the work it sees needs doing *here and now*.

The Aims of the Church: Priorities and Adaptation of Means

What must be done must be done. In order to do what it sees as its duty the Church chooses appropriate means, but its power must also be controlled and it must listen to criticism both from within and without. This should help the Church to become aware of the doubtful value of some of its aims, or of means employed which shock public opinion. If the Church proclaims liberation, it must give an example of freedom and independence from economic and political worldly powers. This means it should reject certain easily available but dubious financial assistance.

The Church's Heritage and Proper Activity in Particular Places

A local church inherits not only spiritual values but worldly goods of which it must give an account and critically review. Often a bad administration of accumulated wealth prevents its useful employment in charitable action. Then the past becomes the means to the alienation of the future, because of the blindness of the present. Let us apply the wisdom of the world to this: a proper adaptation of means to ends, with accounts made public to the faithful who contribute to the common good. They are shocked particularly by frivolous expenditure, incessant useless journey by unstable characters endowed with spiritual powers, the excesses we deplore in the consumer society. Ecclesiastical administration must not make tenants, clients, taxpayers, dependants who hate its power, nor must it support unjust profiteers from its funds.

The Church should prefer voluntary contributions. Of course these are more difficult to raise today in the face of great competition and the fact that they are insecure makes planning more difficult. Although fixed revenues may be indispensable (and for this the tithe system is by far the best), these mean that the Church becomes involved in the socio-economic structure of the country and therefore strict vigilance is required so that its prophetic mission, whose duty it is to oppose this structure, is not paralysed. Administration of community funds only becomes properly christian when it encourages mutual missionary and universal help. Charity is not against realistic planning and accounting; it merely opens it to a wider horizon.

The Threshold beyond which Values Change Significance

The obsession with visible efficiency leading to large-scale investments both in developed and under-developed countries, risks the loss of any real efficacity for the Gospel. At the other extreme, it is difficult for the Gospel message to reach certain areas without considerable material and human resources. Either extreme alone leads to barrenness. A balance must be found. Beyond certain limits all the 'benefits' of civilization are reversed and become actually harmful. The abuse of 'sacralization' has led to an equally radical 'desacralization'. The Church's activity should not be in competition with the secular. It should be directed towards services which secular society is not suited to performing, either because they are outside its scope (education in the faith), or because they happen not to be able to at some particular time (for example education of certain handicapped groups); it should join in the efforts of the whole world when some catastrophe demands massive and immediate relief. But careful attention should always be paid to the rapid altering of situations and priorities. Work which used to bear witness and be important (most work does not bear witness unless it is seen to do good) may cease to do and be so, without the workers' realising it. This means that the work being done and the witness it bears to the Gospel should be tested from time to time by public opinion and its effectiveness judged by outside standards. (This does not of course include applying the standards of the world to financial profits.)

THE CHURCH'S RESPONSIBILITIES NOW

The drive for efficiency loses its point if the quality of human relationships is sacrificed to mere quantity. Justice means extending brotherhood as far as human dominion over the earth extends. Human relationships must never be sacrificed to things, profits, statistics or the whims of the rich. Freedom from the tyranny of 'worldly goods' and also from want means self-discipline, controlling our desires and remaining brothers.

The Church as Institution

Applications of means to ends in the Church cannot be worked out *a priori* because they depend on changing cultural values; they must be continually revised. Democratic organization of community structures helps to see that this revision is properly done. The craze for secrecy and anonymity, the autocratic exercise of power are harmful to the Church's witness and do not even always increase efficiency.

The Church as People of God

Not all lay people are required to be poor, but all must show that they are concerned with justice and that they are prepared to fight

against evil systems. Latin American Catholics should become aware
of the meanness of their contribution towards the Church's expenses.
We know that people are much readier to pay lip service than cash to the
needs of the poor. In rich countries a good diocese is often thought of
as a diocese where the money flows in well. Meanwhile the gap continues to widen between rich and poor countries and also between the
social classes in the developing countries. In Brazil between 1960 and
1970 the richest 10% of the population increased their share of the
country's wealth from 38.87% to 48.35%, while inflation far out-
stripped the rise in wages and also of course increased the poverty of
the unemployed. During the present decade this situation is getting
even worse. Nevertheless those responsible for and benefiting from it
are mainly Catholics anxious to prevent the advent of a Communist
régime. Efficiency is used for selfish ends with a feeble palliative of fine
phrases.

Monks and Nuns

Except for those who have a special vocation, monks and nuns are
not required to be poorer than the poorest. But their individual and
collective life style should show a general austerity, in accordance with
their personal and communal vocations. They must bear witness by
their thrift, careful administration without being either mean or merci-
less, generous sharing, according to their particular sphere of action in
the Church and the world. The right use of the wealth of a religious
community (property, revenue, organization, jurisdiction, influence)
should act as an example of what should be expected in civil society.
Religious communities also normally bear witness to the Gospel by the
good they have done throughout their history. But Jesus himself did not
cure all the sick people in Judaea in his time. Visible results may often
be slight but a life of poverty and detachment freed from worldly excesses is also a sharing in the Kingdom. The slavery of worldly materialism makes people blind. Monks and nuns have the duty to try and
restore their vision. Living in poverty is not an absolute but a verb to be
conjugated in all the persons, voices and modes necessary to freedom in
any particular situation.

Conclusion

We don't have to give up the mysticism which is the tap-root of
Christianity and to which our century also has a right. But we must
de-mystify the way we talk because this has cut off the Church from the
real needs of the world expecting salvation from it. We must speak
plainly and truly, act plainly and truly so that we can bring back the

essential message of the Gospel in a world rushing headlong into technological change. Poverty must not be a trinket displayed under glass by the Church in a few religious orders. Poverty in both its human and its religious context means solidarity, order, *moderation*, whereas the trend of our civilization is towards *excess* (in the use of vast new powers without consideration of their effect on the common good or significance to the world as a whole). Poverty also means a *respectful attitude* to the world. We may use its goods but neither idolise nor ransack them. (This also includes respect for our ecological heritage which we must guard for future generations.) It means the *transcendance of human freedom* above its material and cultural conditioning, and *submission to a Creator* who is Lord of the ultimate goal of history.

The tendency of our industrial and post-industrial civilization is to exhaust the earth's resources by the materialism of its life-style disregarding every law of the Father. The exact point at which Christian witness must re-enter the system of constructive forces in the world is neither an arbitrary nor a pre-determined one.

Translated by Dinah Livingstone

Yves Congar

Poverty as an Act of Faith

I am not concerned here with poverty in the economic sense, which is both complex and difficult to define and a topic which has been treated by many other authors. After all, I lack almost nothing that I need and therefore feel unqualified to write on the subject. I am too well aware of the truth of Georges Bernanos' remark that 'you have to be really wretched yourself in order to participate non-sacrilegiously in the sacrament of wretchedness' (*Project for a Life of Jesus*, 1943).

And I am not concerned with religious poverty from the institutional angle. The criticisms it arouses are well-known, especially Luther's objection that the monks were often better fed, clothed and housed than other people of their time;[1] or Voltaire's of the dowries of girls who were not sufficiently rich to make a vow of poverty. What I wish to say applies to Christian life as such, but just as much to a vow of poverty for the religious life and poverty as accepted in the apostolic life. The three traditional vows comprise several levels of practice. The first level is institutional and legal: obedience consists in following the rule and deciding one's life in obedience to one's superiors (permission); chasity in avoiding the pleasure normally experienced in contact with the other sex; poverty in the acquisition and use of benefits in dependence on one's superiors and within the framework of communal life.

There is a deeper level: that of the actual exercise of the corresponding virtues. That takes one much further. It is a life of *metanoia* lived in a way which everyday demands on one. There is no such thing as a virtue of poverty, but there are certainly virtuous demands concerning the possession and use of everything which one can say one owns—not only money, but health, time, social assistance, a motor car, books, culture, knowledge, and so on. It is the virtues of prudence, liberality, generosity, and in certain aspects those of temperance, which regulate the use of our possessions. But they are gathered up into the thrust of a consecration to living absolutely the love of God and one's neighbour.

In the life of a practising Christian, the Holy Spirit intervenes beyond the area of virtues: by inspiration; by, therefore, impulses towards the evangelical absolute. Then we are very near the third level, where the content of the three traditional vows is lived on the level no longer merely of an ethic, of a human rule (even though Christian) of our relations with things and people, but as a certain quality of existence which deserves the epithet *theologal*.

This is above all true of obedience and poverty which at this level are almost identical in the form of a theologal humility which in itself is both faith and hope. It is an aspect of our life 'coram Deo', before and towards God. It is an aspect of the religious link between ourselves and the living God who revealed himself as our Father in Jesus Christ.

That was experienced in Israel (with difficulty and after a progressive education) by the poor.[2] For that not only the prophets were necessary but Israel through trials and suffering had to lose its human confidence. Poverty, like the 'coram Deo' attitude, became the characteristic of the true faithful. Within a fleshy nation a true people of God appeared— 'that lasting Israel which lives by prayer and expectation . . . longing for encounter with God' (Gelin, p. 98), which was superlatively personified in that young Nazareth girl, Mary; just as Mary's Magnificat is something like a summary of the doxological prayer of the Psalms which express the faith and hope of the people of God: I, God, shall be known in my actions. I shall be with you and for you.

That was the line of theologal truth which Jesus took up in the first beatitude, and which he commented on when he said: 'No one can serve two masters. You cannot serve God and Mammon'—that is, God and money. The Greek transposed this Aramaic word of uncertain etymology but which may be derived from the root '*mn* which gives us the verb '*aman*, to carry, which in the causative means to cause to be borne (one's burden or one's weakness by another), *to lean on*, and therefore, on the spiritual level, *to put one's trust in*.[3] This is the word which means *to believe* in the Hebrew Bible. The crucial question is to know in whom, absolutely and ultimately, one puts one's trust. Is it in Yahweh or in Baal? The Psalms unceasingly celebrate the aid given by Yahweh as against the impotence of idols (cf. Prov. 18:10–11).

This was Péguy's inspiration when he made God the Father reproach the rich 'who do not want to be my creatures', who 'take shelter in being my servants'.[4] That is going too far. It is a question of knowing ultimately if God is (recognized as) God or if one is honouring another in his place. We also find these statements in the captivity Epistles: 'Put to death therefore what is earthly in you . . . and covetousness, which is idolatry' (Col. 3:5); *pleon-exia*, the desire to have more. 'Be sure of this, that no fornicator or impure man, or one who is covetous (that is, an idolator), has any inheritance in the kingdom of Christ and of God'(Eph. 5:5): *pleon-exktes*, he who always wants more. These texts, and the term *avarus, avaritia*, have played a major role in Christian ethics as expressed by the Fathers, the Councils, and the medieval Doctors.[5] We might add 1 Tim. 6:10: 'For the love of money— *philargia*—is the root of all evils'. But Vinet noted in the nineteenth century that no one ever preached a sermon on avarice.[6] If anyone speaks of it nowadays, it is in the context of economic ethics rather than in terms of fundamental theology.[7]

Ultimately it is a question of God being God; that he should be acknowledged as God, and therefore as the absolute Source. For that to come about we have to be aware of our absolute indigence. Luther was not a saint, but he made that conviction the basis of his project: 'Only the lost sheep is looked for, only the prisoner is released, only the poor man is enriched, only the sick man is strengthened, only the humbled is exalted, only the empty is filled, only that which was not is built up.'[8] And there are more pure texts, more God-centered ones, and many of them, in Thérèse of Lisieux: 'What pleases him (God) is to see me liking my lowliness and my poverty, it is the blind hope that I have in his mercy . . . We have to agree to stay poor without pressure' (letter to her sister Marie du Sacré-Coeur, 17 September 1896); 'On the eve of this life I shall appear before you with empty hands, because I do not ask you Lord to number my works. All our just dues are inadequacies in your eyes' *(Act of consecration to merciful Love)*.

The absolute model is of course Jesus Christ in the perfection of his filial spirit. Jesus always said that *everything* was due to his Father. 'My teaching is not mine, but his who sent me' (Jn. 7:16; cf. 8:28). It is not only a Johannine theme but the basis of the hymn in Phil. 2:6–11. The kenosis and obedience of one who is of God is poverty experienced actually within divinity: not only in Jesus through the Incarnation, but by the Word in that absolute state of dependence in which he is of the Father, Principle without principle, the Source of divinity. It was on a 'metaphysics of the saints' drawn from this theology that Bérulle grounded a spirituality of dependence and adoration: 'a nothing in the hands of God, a nothing destined for God, a nothing referred to God'.[9]

To take this road is to share in the mystery of Christ and therefore in God's intention for the world, his wisdom. The theme of the poor man as wise has hardly received due attention. Bonaventure mentioned it in passing: the poor man is wise because he despises the world, in the sense of preferring God absolutely, who counts absolutely.[10] There are

statements closer to actual experience in the testimonies to the rediscovery of poverty in the modern Church, after the last War and just
before and during the Council.[11] First there was a certain degree of
shock on becoming aware of the poverty of the masses—in the missions
to the workers, among the worker priests and so on. House groups
added to their family spirituality the ideal and practice of sharing things
in common. A number of movements held meetings on, and journals
devoted issues to, poverty, and a spirituality of poverty developed.[12]
The Third World was discovered: the reality of poverty. Charles de
Foucauld was an influence, together with other religious movements.
Emmanuel Mounier's work was very representative of this trend and,
in the best sense, exemplary. He wrote in 1933: 'Men share with one
another according to whether they have or have not realized the misery
of the world today.' Two days before his sudden death, he confided in
Père Depierre his desire to rejoin the poor.[13] He had just written: 'My
Gospel is the Gospel of the poor. It will never allow me to accept the
slightest misunderstanding with those who are in the confidence of the
poor. I shall never take any pleasure in what can divide the world and
the hope of the poor.'

This rediscovery of poverty as a value in the Christian life occurred
spontaneously on the social level. That is certainly connected with the
present context of social Catholicism, of openness to the world, of
solidarity with human suffering, but there is a deeper connection (at the
heart of the theologal tension and by way of inward demands) between
existing for God and existing for mankind. The two are inseparable.
The second commandment is not merely like the first, but *identical* with
it. The Bible does not talk about God without talking about man, and
vice versa. It is indivisibly theology for man and anthropology for God.

This logic is clear in the life of Francis of Assisi, who as far as
poverty is concerned, deserves to be called 'first after the Unique', as
Allo said of St Paul. The starting-point comes at the beginning of his
conversion to the evangelical life. Francis had just abandoned a life of
prodigality. His father Peter of Bernadone wanted to put an end to it
and to save what was left of his money. Francis took all his clothes and
put them together with the money at his father's feet and said: 'Listen
and understand. Until now I called Peter of Bernadone my father. But
since I have decided to serve God alone henceforth, I am giving back to
Peter of Bernadone the money he was so worried about and all the
clothes I got from him. From now on I shall be able to say; not "My
father Peter of Bernadone", but "Our Father who art in heaven".[14]
Obviously such a gesture is only rendered authentic and just by unrelenting devotion to a divine absolute. Francis' poverty was essentially

theologal as the exercise of an absolute vertical dependence on the
Father who cares for men, flowers and animals.[15]

That is why this vertical relationship transforms horizontal relations.
The second beatitude concerns the tender. We are aware of the part
played in Francis' life by preaching to the birds, by the Canticle of
creation, by the episode of the robbers, but there is another inference.[16]
A brother thought a psalter was needed. Francis refused and told him:
'When you have a psalter, you will want a breviary. When you have a
breviary you will sit on a throne like a great prelate and say to your
brother: Fetch my breviary!' That shows how owning things is the root
of the spirit of domination; it corrupts the human heart and destroys the
truth of fraternal feeling. Christianity struggled against it for some time.
It lost out when money left the context of direct personal property to
find a new location in impersonal economic structures, requiring a new
development of ethics and a transition to the level of politics. But whatever happens the important thing is the human heart and its respect for
poverty, and three gifts of great price: openness, a giving disposition,
essential hope.

In the lives of people like Francis and in our own times, Dorothy
Day, Emmanuel Mounier, Father Christian, it is striking how evangelical poverty brings openness and availability. It breaks down the
screens which prevent us from being fraternal, wholly open to others
and with them. 'After a bombing raid (during the war), we could talk to
one another in the street! Every passer-by was a brother in suffering.
What the raids most obviously pulled down were the walls in people's
hearts. How wonderful it was to see people talking to one another. But
first they had to become poor. Once the war was over people began to
pretend not to know one another all over again. They were solicitors or
labourers once more'.[17]

It is a fact of experience: the poor give more, and more easily, than
the rich. It is not only in Victor Hugo that they take in the child of a
dead neighbour or someone who is ill, even though it means adding to
their own family. Here is a tale from a very real world: 'I have never
seen anything more beautiful in the world than Rio de Janeiro. To
arrive there at night is marvellous. In this magnificent city more than a
million out of three and a half million live in poverty and misery in the
shanty towns. At the heart of Moro shanty town I entered one of the
shacks. A woman alone with three children was stretched out, seriously ill. I stayed for fifteen minutes. In this short time three people
came to bring something . . . spontaneously, only because the sick
woman and her children were in need: one brought fruit; another a little
soup; the third a little rice in water . . . The last of the three told us that

was her evening meal, and that as a result she would have nothing to eat that night.

I was struck by these three visits: "The poor are good . . . the poor are good . . ." These visits, these offerings, this spontaneity, this love, were surely the same as those shown by the shepherds. I think that then I understood better why God had invited them to the first Christmas and why he did not invite the others.'[18]

These were the real poor, both economically and in the gospel sense. There are also poor people who have a rich person's soul. They think only of receiving, and do not know how to give. But a rich man can have the soul of a poor person. It is almost miraculous.

The poor are bearers of hope. Of course they could be wiped out and not survive in anything but an unconscious state, by animal instinct; but the poor with spiritual awareness look to the future. In so doing they become an historical force, even though at present they may be powerless. It was in the midst of setbacks and in a countryside marked by troops and invasion that the little people of the poor of God, such as Mary, Anna and Simeon, awaited the consolation of Israel. Ultimately it is poverty which opens up the ways of the future. There is a link between poverty and prophecy.[19] Also between poverty and childhood, under the double and mutual sign of indigence and hope. And also: 'If you do not become as little children . . .' Pure like children (though today they are not so pure), obedient like children, poor like children dependent and trusting as they are directed to the future in hope . . .

APOSTOLIC POVERTY

Poverty seen and lived as absolute dependence on God the Father and as a condition of fraternal availability is the disposition most appropriate to what God requires for his creation. It is always apparent in God's behaviour. For instance in the history of Israel there in Gideon and the incident in which God reduced the host to a handful 'lest Israel vaunt themselves against me, saying: "My own hand has delivered me" (Judg. 7:2). There is the occasion when young David confronted the giant Goliath: 'You come to me with a sword, and with a spear and with a javelin; but I come to you in the name of the Lord God of hosts, the God of the armies of Israel, whom you have defied . . . all the earth may know that there is a God in Israel, and all this assembly . . . may know that the Lord saves not with sword and spear . . .' (1 Sam. 17:45–7). When we get to St Paul, the testimonies abound, both in the accounts of his apostolate and in his own writings, that the power of God is given in full in human weakness: cf 2 Cor. 12:7–10; 1 Cor. 2:1–5.

It is not our own work. It is bread asked for daily and given daily. The law of the instrumental cause is to give what it does not possess.[20] Bernanos' country priest is well able to bear witness thus: 'O miracle of our empty hands!' There is here a kind of dialectic, a paradox to which there is probably no satisfactory intellectual solution, but which is resolved by life: the saints have sought an effective course and have used means available to them; at the same time they have expected God to use his power in the midst of desertion, opposition and a lack of resources and strength.

One of the laws of apostolic endeavour is indifference to possession and non-possession. As soon as the apostle is in the midst of plenty, surrounded by friends, he is destitute. Elisha had a comfortable room at the Shunammite woman's house, and an easy life (2 Kgs., 4:8). The same was true of Jesus at Bethany but at other times he was on the road without anything, with nowhere to sleep, and having to face hostility. St Paul in Malta was very well treated (Acts 28:7-10?, but he experienced prison, blows, hunger, cold, shipwreck, and disloyalty (2 Cor. 11:23-7). He himself stated the law of *apostolic* poverty: 'I have learned, in whatever state I am, to be content. I know how to be abased, and I know how to abound; in any and all circumstances I have learned the secret of facing plenty and hunger, abundance and want. I can do all things in him who strengthens me' (Phil. 4:11-3). That is not stoicism but apostolic theology.

That is the condition of total availability to men and circumstances. The rich will always have an excuse for escaping it (cf Mt. 8:18-22 and 19:22 par.; Lk. 14:15-24). Paul on the other hand proudly declares the freedom of his apostolic life and his conditions of life: 'For though I am free from all men, I have made myself a slave to all, that I might win the more . . . I have become all things to all men . . .' (1 Cor. 9:19-22). Apostolic poverty is availability, without any self-affirmation, offering oneself to others, to circumstances, and to the action of God in the midst of all that. That is not only a law for individuals but for the Church in its human institutions. The history of the mission bears witness to that in showing that sometimes the missionaries were Jews among the Jews, without the law among those without the law, but that at other times the retention of a tradition without allowing it to be questioned nullified the whole enterprise.

That shows us that the purest spiritual phenomenon has an impact in the temporal sphere, but also, in order to prove itself true, looks to certain socio-economic or cultural presuppositions. We have already seen how, since God is the Father of all, the theologal context demanded fraternal behaviour in the social context. We now see that apostolic availability realizes the demands of *metanoia* even at the level of structures, government, the exercise of ownership, and so on. A soul needs its body but a body is even more in need of its soul. The problem of applying the evangelical counsels on poverty to the Church as such, as people that is, but above all as institution, is a very delicate one.[21]

Translated by V. Green

Notes

1. Sermon of June 5, 1535: WA 41:200.
2. See A. Causse, *Les Pauvres d'Israël* (Paris/Strasbourg, 1922); A. Gelin, *Les Pauvres de Yahvé* (Paris, 1953).
3. This etymology of Mammon is defended by E. Hoskyns and N. Davey in *The Riddle of the New Testament* (third ed., London, 1947), p. 28 n.; and by F. Hauck in *ThWNT*, vol. IV, pp. 390–92.
4. *Le Porche du Mystère de la Deuxième Vertu*, Pléiade edition, p. 171; NRF edition, p. 18.
5. Since there is no full treatment of the subject as far as I am aware, see M. W. Bloomfield, *The Seven Deadly Sins* (East Lansing, 1952); L. K. Little, 'Pride goes before Avarice: Social Change and the Vices in Latin Christendom', in *The American Historical Review*, 76 (1971), pp. 16–49.
6. A. Vinet, *Théologie Pastorale* (Paris, 1889), pp. 155 ff.
7. Cf. D. Villey, J. Lebret and P. Bigo, 'L'Avarice et le monde de l'argent', in *Monde moderne et sens du Péché* (Paris, 1956), pp. 85–126. See also my own article on poverty in the Christian life in *Concilium*, 1966.
8. *Scholie sur Rom.* 3: 7; ed. Ficker, II, pp. 57–8; WA 56, p. 218.
9. *Correspondance*, ed. Dagens, vol. III, p. 314.
10. *In Ecclesiasten: Opera Quaracchi*, VI, p. 52[b].
11. The history of the renewal of Christian poverty has still to be written. There are a few pages on the subject and an extensive bibliography in Aquinata Böckmann, *Die Armut in der inner-kirchlichen Diskussion heute* (Münsterschwarzach, 1973).
12. See the books by P.-R. Regamey, 1941, 1963 *(La Pauvreté et l'homme d'aujourd'hui)*, 1967.
13. Cf. André Depierre, 'Ce témoin persévérant de Dieu', in *Esprit*, December 1950, pp. 905–22.
14. Bonaventura, *Legenda Major*, c. 2; J. Joergensen, *Saint François d'Assise*, ch. vii (Paris, 1912), p. 68.
15. See my 'Saint François ou l'Absolu de l'Evangile en chrétienté', in *Les Voies du Dieu vivant* (Paris, 1962), pp. 247–64. Cf. from the viewpoint of

evangelical *metanoia*, 'De armoede van Sint Franciscus en het heilig Evangelie', in *Sint Franciscus,* 57 (1955), pp. 41–208. References to the texts of the Sermon on the Mount in *Regula non bullata*, ed. Boehmer, *Analekten z. Gesch. des Fr. v. As.* (Tübingen & Leipzig, 1906), no. 14, p. 13 ff.

16. *Legenda antiqua,* pp. 69–79; ed. F. Delorme, 1926, pp. 40–42; *Speculum perfectionis*, ed. P. Sabatier, p. 11.

17. L. Evely, *Our Father* (New York & London, 1958).

18. J. Bouchaud, *Les pauvres m'ont évangélisé* (Paris, 1968), p. 14.

19. P. Ganne, *Le pauvre et le prophète* (Cultures et Foi, Lyon, no. 28–9, Summer, 1973): a politico-religious approach.

20. T. Chifflot, 'L'avoir, condition de la créature', in *Rev. Sc. ph. th., 28* (1939), pp. 40–57.

21. I have studied the problem in the symposium *Eglise et Pauvreté (Unam Sanctam 57)* (Paris, 1965), pp. 135–55.

Victor Conzemius

Solidarity of European Priests

DURING the discussion of the decree on the pastoral tasks of bishops in the Church in November 1963, Bishop Marcelin Gonzalez Martin of Astorga (now Cardinal Archbishop of Toledo) stated the need for a fair distribution of funds throughout the universal Church. The faithful would be shocked if they were aware of the inadequacies of the means and incomes of priests in different countries and areas even in one country, and even in the same diocese. The discrepancies prevent many otherwise possible actions on the part of the clergy and con-tradict the social function of property which is continually emphasized in theory. In practice the Church keep firmly to a narrow conception of private property even in regard to the arrangement of its own material needs.

The appeal to do away with this class spirit in the Church raises such a number of difficulties in practice that only a very few steps have been taken in the right direction. Here I shall touch on only one aspect of the range of problems raised by Gonzalez: an equitable redistribution of means among priests. In countries where the payment of the clergy nowadays has largely become a matter of individual improvization, as the result of a strict separation of Church and state, everyone is con-scious of the need for a general measure. By introducing a standard income (nevertheless still far from the minimum living wage) some French dioceses have tried to overcome the worst discrepancies.

I do not intend to examine the fundamental question of how the support of the clergy within a country or region should be organized. I start from the basic experience that ten years after the Council there is still great inequality in the stipends and pay of priests. In Europe too there are privileged and under-privileged dioceses. The dividing-line should not be drawn between payment by the state and church taxes on the one hand, and voluntary disbursements by the faithful on the other. Even in the socialist countries there are urban priests who are privileged earners in comparison with the priests of small country parishes. On the other hand, in countries which are especially favoured by the great economic divide, such as Switzerland, there can be inequalities in clergy stipends which no one outside would think possible. In the dioceses of Tessin, Wallis and Fribourg-Lausanne-Geneva, clergy stipends in some parishes are at the lowest possible living wage. Only in the last few years have compensatory funds been set up to assimilate clergy incomes to one another within a diocese or canton.

The inequality is much more striking and scandalous if one compares certain European countries. Whereas in the German-speaking countries anyone working for the Church is well looked after and belongs to a privileged class in society as a whole, a priest in France or Italy is in a more than precarious position. Priests in one country can enjoy all the comforts of civilized living, whereas others can hardly get together the money they need to cure their tuberculosis. Not only are living, housing and working conditions different, but health insurance or social security and old age pension arrangements are so underdeveloped in different areas, that priests are among the underprivileged.

The question arises whether the fate of one priest decreed by socio-cultural accident should not be borne by another out of free solidarity. A distant goal worth striving for would be an equalization fund for priests and their colleagues in the service of the Church. Since the organizational means are at present lacking, a 'solidarity fund' should be started first. It would be set up by voluntary surrender of a certain portion of income and of mass stipends or similar receipts. The voluntary aspect should be retained. Publicity would be managed through priests' councils, which would also decide the distribution of the funds. Basically no projects should be supported but only human beings (cost of living, pension funds, sick funds) who live to do their apostolic duty. Distribution could be effected through the secretariat of the European bishops' conference, so that the establishment of a new 'organization' would be avoided.

Perhaps some will object that this proposal would compete with existing initiatives. They overlook the fact that this kind of fraternal assistance would help the missions above all, where the material need of priests is usually still greater. In fact there are already several initiatives which have as their goal the support of priests in European countries or in young churches. First place in this regard is taken by the aid provided for priests in eastern Europe by Fr Werenfried van Straaten's organization. Then in Germany there is a body of former students of the German College helping certain Italian dioceses. In Switzerland there is an aid organization for the same purpose which is largely supported by the faithful. For a number of years priests in Belgian dioceses and the diocese of Luxembourg have contributed a kind of 'self-tax' in order to pay the social security contributions of their colleagues who are working as *Fidei Donum* priests in missionary dioceses. In Germany there is the major effort of PRIM (Priests in the Missions) which is supported by the priests' councils and contributed to by a good third of all priests. It has become a fixture providing real assistance in areas of ecclesiastical need and in the poorest countries of the world as indicated by UNCTAD. Since its foundation in 1970 until 1975 nearly seven million DM were paid out for various aid projects.

My proposal is not intended to compete with or exclude such initiatives, but only to extend them by reminding everyone that priests in European areas of need should also be included in this fraternal aid. The need in Europe is not so obvious as in developing countries. But there is shocking poverty among European priests which is not so publicly known because it is kept dark by local churches for national or other prestige reasons. The churches' initiative in the missionary areas should not let us forget that there are great inadequacies in Europe. The public should first be made aware of the situation by appropriate documentation. The European trade unions have a fund which they draw on in certain cases to help countries which are in situations of political or financial crisis. Until now the European clergy have not succeeded in organizing that kind of solidarity fund. This is an opportunity to see such a partnership not only in terms of financial aid but to make it a means of personal encounter and exchange. At a time when we are striving for European unity, the clergy could offer an example of the suppression of national egotisms which in the past the Church so often helped to confirm. The spiritual readiness and truth required in this instance is much more demanding and difficult than that which appears in socio-political theory or in spectacular actions for the Third World. It requires a willingness to learn and to exchange which is not easily arrested by reference to the complete difference of socio-cultural traditions. The European priests' councils and bishops' conferences should have the courage to act in this regard. Ultimately, their actions will be to the advantage of the universal Church.

A Group of Bishops

Thirteen Commitments

JUST before the close of the second Vatican Council, an unknown number of anonymous bishops who had formed part of a larger body discussing the poor in the Church and the poor Church, made public the following declaration:

We bishops who have come together at the Vatican Council, having realized the deficiencies of our life of poverty in accordance with the Gospel, and having been mutually encouraged in an endeavour in which each of us wishes to avoid individuality and presumption; united with all our brothers in the episcopate; counting above all on the power and grace of our Lord Jesus Christ, on the prayers of the faithful and the priests of our respective dioceses; placing ourselves in thought and prayer before the Trinity, before the Church of Christ, before the priests and faithful of our dioceses, in humility and awareness of our weakness, but also with all the determination and strength which God grants us, we commit ourselves to the following:

1. We shall try to live in the ordinary manner of our population, in matters of housing, food, means of travel, and all that appertains thereto (Mt. 5:3; 6:33–34; 8:20).

2. We henceforth renounce the appearance and the reality of riches, especially in clothing (fine cloth, striking colours), insignia in precious materials (for these signs should be evangelical: Mk. 6:9; Mt. 10:9; Acts 3:6).

3. We shall possess neither dwelling nor furniture, nor bank accounts and so on, in our own names; if possessions are necessary, we shall put everything in the name of the diocese or social or charitable organizations (Mt. 6:19–21; Lk. 12:33–34).

4. Whenever possible, we shall entrust the financial and material administration of our dioceses to a committee of lay people who are competent and aware of their apostolic rôle, so that we can be less administrators and more pastors and apostles (Mt. 10:8; Acts 6:17).

5. We shall refuse to be addressed orally or in writing by names and titles indicating importance and power (Eminence, Excellence, Monsignor). We prefer to be addressed by the evangelical title Father.

6. We shall avoid in our behaviour and social relations anything which might seem to give privileges, priorities or even any kind of preference to the rich and powerful (for instance, banquets given or accepted, social classes in religious services) (Lk. 13:12–4; 1 Cor. 9:14–19).

7. Similarly we shall avoid encouraging or flattering the vanity of any person with a view to rewarding or soliciting gifts, or for any other reason. We shall ask the faithful to consider their gifts as normal participation in worship, the apostolate and social action (Mt. 6:2–4; Lk. 15:9–13; 2 Cor. 12–14).

8. We shall give all that is required of our time, thought, heart, means and so forth to the apostolic and pastoral service of working and economically weak and under-developed individuals and groups, but without injuring other persons and groups in the diocese. We shall support the laity, religious, deacons or priests whom the Lord summons to evangelize the poor and workers by sharing working life and labour (Lk. 4:18; Mk. 6:4; Mt. 11:45; Acts 18:3–4; 20:33–35; 1 Cor. 4:12; 9:1–27).

9. Aware of the demands of justice and charity and of their connections, we shall try to change works of 'charity' into social works based on charity and justice, which take into account everyone and all demands, as humble service to the competent public bodies (Mt. 25:31–46; Lk. 13:12–14, 33–34).

10. We shall take all measures possible to ensure that those responsible in our governments and public services pass and apply laws, structures and social institutions which are needed for justice, equality and the equitable and total development of man as a whole in all men, and thereby for the attainment of a new social order worthy of sons of men and sons of God (Acts 2:44–45; 4:32–35; 5:4; 2 Cor. 8 and 9 *in toto;* 1 Tim. 5:16).

11. Since the collegiality of bishops is realized in its most evangelical form in common responsibility for those masses who live in a state of physical, cultural and mental misery (two-thirds of humanity), we commit ourselves: to share according to our means in the urgent investments of the episcopates of the poor nations; to solicit together, at the level of international organizations, but in witnessing to the Gospel,

like Pope Paul VI at the United Nations, the establishment of economic and cultural structures which no longer produce proletarian nations in a world of the increasingly rich, but which allow the poor masses to emerge from their misery.

12. We commit ourselves to share in pastoral love our lives with our brothers in Christ, priests, religious and laity, so that our ministry may be a true service; hence: we shall try to 'revise our lives' together with them; we shall encourage co-workers so that we inspire according to the Spirit rather than administer according to the world; we shall try to be more humanly present and welcoming; we shall show ourselves as open to all, whatever their religion (Mk. 8:34–35; Acts 6:1–7; 1 Tim. 3:8–10).

13. When we return to our respective dioceses, we shall inform our diocesan bishops of our resolution, and ask them to help us through their understanding, co-operation and prayers.

May God help us to be faithful!

Alois Müller

The Poor and the Church: A Synthesis

THE number of Christian attitudes to poverty may seem rather odd. But even conceptual precision is difficult in this regard. The authors of this issue of *Concilium* found this an overriding problem, and could not in the end offer the reader an absolutely straightforward view and definition of the notion. One might suppose that the 'Church of the poor' was actually a catchphrase for a host of problems which are not wholly interconnected. If we really want to reach a balanced view and synthesis in this area, we are perhaps promising to do more than an article could ever manage on the topic. But it is worth trying.

THE MAIN LINES OF THE PROBLEM

First we must underline the many-sidedness of the term 'poverty'. It can refer to misery, or to a severe threat to life itself, or to a form of imprisonment. It can indicate material impoverishment but also freedom and happiness; it can signify a social condition of withdrawal and powerlessness, of marginality leading to spiritual suffering; and it can of course refer to something theologically quite respectable: a condition of union with, or relatedness to, God.

The question is: if these ideas are not synonymous, then is there a definite connection between them? Is one kind of poverty to be shunned and opposed; and another followed? If so; which in each case? Are they mutually exclusive, or is it a matter of Christian paradox, so that the undesirable poverty is the one worth fighting for? What definite meaning can we attribute to the phase 'Church of the poor'? We can at least point out certain tendencies.

The Church must help redress poverty. There is full agreement that that is the case in regard to poverty as physical deprivation and misery, where a lack causes severe suffering and makes a life worthy of a human being impossible. But that is also true of the poverty which consists of social discrimination and neglect, whether conditioned by lack of means or by other factors. Wherever this form of poverty is in question the Church has to be the Church of the poor in the sense that it frees the poor from such poverty. To that extent the Christian notion seems identical not only with the Marxist but with that form of western liberal thought which intends the greatest possible prosperity for the greatest possible number of people. But that implies another demand.

Before all else the Christian notion requires solidarity with the poor. This solidarity is not synonymous with the eradication of poverty. Christians should be on the side of the poor because 'the world' is not on their side, and because like all men and women—they are divinely constituted to be worthy of having others on their side. That very co-operation with the poor is the Christian value in question.

This solidarity is also co-operation and help wherever the poor have to be assisted: that is, wherever poverty implies a form of misery. Helping the poor means freeing them when their poverty is unfreedom. The Church of the poor can only exist in solidarity with the poor if it is a poor Church. Verbal solidarity alone is not real solidarity.

That raises another insistent question. Is there a value in being poor? Poverty that is not misery, suffering and so on, is often equated with freedom and openness to the future. If that is so, then there is a poverty that ought not to be banished. 'The Poor Church' is not then a transient measure intended to help one 'reach' the poor but in this case the Church approaches the poor in the condition of itself being the poor, so that it can teach the poor about a poverty which is valuable in itself.

The Church also consists of the poor when the poor become the Church and the Church does not have to become poor. But do the poor have to become the Church? Surely, as the poor, they are already the people of God? Of course the good news is for the poor. But for the sake of that good news they are the people of God, and not for the sake of some socio-political idea. The poverty which makes us open for God's message of fraternity is valuable in its own right.

Here we reach the final dimension of poverty—the 'theological'. Poverty as the emptiness that would be filled by God is the poverty which is glorified, and called happy. The question is how it relates to any other form of poverty. In the Gospel sense it ought to have its best opportunity where an individual or a church is not already 'filled' with other goods—with material, psychological, social and cultural possessions.

Of course we must not overlook the fact that a poor Church of the poor cannot simply divest itself of all material goods. Yet it is important to remember that the 'means' must be in proportion to the end—not only quantitatively but qualitatively: in the part they play, in the ways in which they are used and applied.

After all the foregoing, perhaps we can after all try to elicit a consistent even though complex 'doctrine' of the Church and poverty.

GUIDELINES FOR CHRISTIAN PRACTICE

An essential insight for the Christian in this regard is the knowledge that riches and impoverishment are both forms of restriction from which people have to free themselves or to be freed. Of course the two things are not symmetrical. A person *strives for* riches whereas he *falls into* poverty. The impoverished experiences his condition as need and bonds, but the rich man is rarely aware of that. Therefore the poor man waits to be freed from his circumstances, whereas the rich man would rather defend himself against that. Hence there is a dual imperative for the Christian and the Church: to free itself from the bonds of riches and to free the poor man from the bonds of impoverishment. The one root of this dual imperative is human freedom to oneself, to one's human being and to one's fellow man. Hence riches as an alternative to poverty cannot be a goal for the Christian. It is obvious today that inhumanity can be produced by striving towards the goal of ever-greater possessions and consumption. Impoverishment should not be replaced by excess; excess is not permissible for the Christian as an economico-political goal. *Pleonexia* or always-wanting-more is the alienating element here and this inclination or habit always comes before excess.

The Christian and the Church find their natural place with the poor. The poor man or woman is the disadvantaged; the one from whom people withdraw, on whose company no one puts any value, whom they would rather have nothing to do with. That however was a yardstick that God shattered in Jesus. Hence for a Christian a poor man or woman is the person for whom one is looking; without whose company one cannot be; the person whose company is not undesirable but welcome. Wherever that happens the poor person has already received the good news; he has already to some extent been freed from poverty—insofar as poverty is alienation.

But, insofar as he lives with the poor, a Christian must free the poor *to* poverty, to the extent that poverty is freedom and wisdom. In poverty there is a temptation to strive for riches, and to adopt the yardstick of the powerful. Solidarity shows the poor that in non-possession they enjoy a greater freedom, and one they ought not to barter. There is a fine tension between these two aspects of the matter. That poverty, as freedom and wisdom, can serve as an alibi to sanction poverty as alienation, is something that Christians must never forget. On the other hand they must never forget that the struggle against poverty as alienation is often in danger of implicitly depending on the yardstick of the 'class enemy', and thereby of negating liberated poverty as an ideal. The fact that the tension is never quite resolved and that any position can be called unilateral is no reason for surrendering the dual position, as long as the task remains of deciding to how far poverty is alienating and how far it is liberating. If the Church does not go over to the poor in order to exist in solidarity with them, and the poor people of a society are the Church, these poor people get their Gospel from Jesus Christ, together with confidence to fight their alienation and love their freedom.

But what is the political relevance of a Church of the poor? It has been said that in the communities of the early Church the problem of the world's shape, of influence outside those communities, was not yet a matter for concern. It was not only foreign to Christians but to society. Yet the situation was not without social relevance. Corinthians I, James and other writings show that within the Christian communities there was confrontation between rich and poor, between masters and slaves; and that it often involved real conflict. Insofar as the poor awaited freedom and the rich found their support in poverty, social change (fraternity) occurred within the limits of the possible. Not the fraternity of the poor against the rich but the fraternity of the poor *and* the rich is the solution which enables the rich to cease to be 'rich' and the poor to stop being 'poor', so that all can find one another in that poverty which is freedom: poverty without need as an alternative to obsessive riches.

The socially relevant means arise from the goal and from the social situation. According to whether one wants a mere reversal of above and below, or fraternity and freedom from need for all men and women, certain means will be found appropriate and practicable, others not. Political effectiveness and action on the part of the Church can emerge from its solidarity with the poor, and in accordance with its complex structure. But we must remember the danger of seeing poverty only in the framework of the class struggle, as if it existed only as socio-economic exploitation. There are and there always will be socially-disadvantaged poor people, for reasons which are not primarily and often not even secondarily conditioned by the social order. It is enough in this regard to think of the disadvantages of physical or mental injuries and their psycho-social consequences. Or will children in the classless society no longer tease an odd or eccentric classmate? That these forms of poverty have always existed is the decisive reason why people for centuries have seen poverty as a divine visitation. Are these particular kinds of poor people to be left as they are, as being of no interest to the class struggle? Or are they to be used for the purposes of the class struggle; if that is the case, then they will suffer the fate of alienating poverty twice over. Christian communities should never sacrifice their fraternal closeness to such people for the sake of a systematic concept.

What, after the foregoing, are we to make of the theological inspiration of poverty? What is the fundamental trust of the poor in God? Is it waiting for a day X when, as in the fairy tale, poverty will be changed to riches? No. Is it the prospect that the sufferings of this time will be as nothing in comparison with the joys that we shall know then (cf. Rom. 8:8)? That is certainly also the case, for this kind of quantified hope is the assurance that we take divine transcendence seriously. It is also the condition ensuring that the following is no illusion: the trust of the poor man in God means that in his necessity he knows and is convinced that God's yardstick, and not the yardstick of 'having', determines every possible true existential value. That gives life its unrestricted freedom. The necessity of the poor man can offer illumination; it is much more difficult for the man who has many possessions, or seeks to have them.

The struggle to overcome misery, impoverishment and alienating poverty must also have a certain spiritual depth which comes from God, and therefore refers to men who are free for the sake of God; in 'secular' terms we might put it thus: it intends the man who acknowledges and realizes his inalienable dignity and does not subordinate it to material values and goals—whether as crass as material possessions or as subtle as political ideologies.

In this perspective, the Church has to be the Church of the poor, so that the struggle for the sake of the poor is in fact their liberation to freedom *from* misery and *to* the freedom of poverty in the good sense.

CONCLUSION

If there is one inspiration of Vatican II which is waiting to be realized, it is the idea of the Church of the poor in this extended sense.

The churches of the rich countries are largely under the shadow of the welfare ideology, and consider it to be the solution to the problem of poverty. But here they do no more than continually reproduce the attitudes which make riches and poverty so enslaving. In addition to the normal psycho-sociological difficulty of not sharing the high standard of living of a society of excessive consumption, these churches endanger their mission by equivocally mixing the principle of pastoral efficiency with the principle of means and power. The new limits of social growth and the inadequacies of the Church perhaps offer an opportunity for a change of mind which we hope will not be ignored. In Latin America decisive new models appear to be emerging in the light of a new theological self-interpretation. They could show the future way for the Church if the basis of their faith, less fragile than that of the second western Enlightenment, survives the encounter with Marxism as ideology.

And what about the young churches of Africa and Asia? It is important that they should go their own way. Perhaps the opportunities before them are greater inasmuch as they have not yet experienced the division of their societies into a minority of exploiters and a majority of the exploited, and do not yet know the bonds of a universal excess of goods in a society in which nothing but consumption counts.

These churches should see their mission as ensuring that they take neither one nor the other wrong road, but instead become truly fraternal societies.

Translated by John Maxwell

Contributors

FERNANDO BASTOS DE AVILA, S.J., was born in Rio de Janeiro, Brazil. He was Vice-Rector of the Catholic University of Rio de Janeiro, where he started a Department of Sociology and Economics and a review in the field of politics, economics and sociology. He has published works on the economic aspects of migration, neo-capitalism and socialism and Christian social thought.

AQUINATA BÖCKMANN, O.S.B., was born in Münster, Germany. Since 1973 she has lectured in moral theology at the papal Regina Mundi Institute associated with the Gregorian University in Rome, and since 1974 she has been professor at the Benedictine St Anselmo Academy. She has published a major work on religious poverty.

MARIE-DOMINIQUE CHENU, O.P. is professor at the Faculty of Catholic Theology, Paris. Among his works is a major study of theology in the twelfth century.

YVES CONGAR, O.P., was born in Sedan, France. He is a member of the International Theological Commission. Among his many major works is a study of salvation and liberation.

VICTOR CONZEMIUS was born in Luxembourg. He is professor of church history in the Theology Faculty of Lucerne University, Switzerland. Among his publications is an edition of the correspondence of Lord Acton and Döllinger.

GUSTAVO GUTIERREZ was born in Lima, Peru. His best-known work among many studies of Latin American pastoral theology is *A Theology of Liberation*. He is professor at the Catholic University of Lima, Peru.

HUBERT LEPARGNEUR was born in Paris. He has taught at various Institutes of philosophy and theology in Brazil since 1958. Among his recent works are a study of the Brazilian Indians and the first volume of a major work on medicine and ethics.

JÓZSEF LUKÁCS was born in Budapest. He holds a chair of philosophy at the Eötvös Lorand University in Budapest. He has taken part in many Christian-Marxist dialogues and published a number of works on the theory of religions.

MICHEL MOLLAT has conducted, since 1962, a research seminar on the poor and poverty in the Middle Ages. Among his works is *The Popular Revolutions of the Late Middle Ages* (London, 1973).

ALOIS MÜLLER was born in Basle, Switzerland. Since 1973 he has been professor of pastoral theology at the University of Lucerne, Switzerland. Among his publications is a study of priests as marginal social figures.

RONALDO MUNOZ was born in Santiago de Chile. His Ratisbon thesis on the new consciousness of the Church in Latin America was published in Chile in 1973.

WERNER POST was born in Balve, Westphalia, Germany. He has lectured on social philosophy since 1972 at a College of Education in Bonn. Among his many works are a study of religion and Karl Marx and an introduction to the theory of materialism.

YORICK SPIEGEL was born in Düsseldorf, Germany. He has been professor of social ethics in Frankfurt-am-Main since 1972. Among his publications are studies of the theology of civil society, the process of mourning and the psychoanalytical exegesis of biblical texts.

KLAUS WINGER was born in Walkenried, Germany. Since 1975 he has been inspector of studies at a theological seminary.